Buster's
Dino Dilemma

ISBN 979-11-86701-03-4 14740

Longtail Books

For the Walmsley family

Chapter 1

"We're here!" Buster shouted.

The **rest** of Mr. Ratburn's third-grade class **cheer**ed.

They were **riding** in a school bus entering Rainbow Rock **State** Park. The class had come there for a field **trip**. The park was a great place to hunt for **fossil**s of **ancient** animals— **including dinosaur**s.

As the bus **pull**ed **to a stop**, Mr. Ratburn stood up.

"After we **exit** the bus," he said, "please **line up** outside in an **orderly fashion**."

The kids **pile**d out quickly. The word *orderly* did not seem to be on anyone's mind.

Binky **leap**t out onto the **pavement**. He **claw**ed at the air. *"T. rex.*★ Grrr!"

Francine lowered her head at him and **stamp**ed her foot. "Triceratops.✱ Raarrr!"

Buster and Arthur stepped around these **fierce beast**s.

"I can't believe we're here!" said Buster.

"I can't believe you keep saying that," said Arthur.

"Well, I'm excited. I've been **count**ing the hours, the minutes, the seconds. . . . I can't wait to get started."

Buster had become very interested in dinosaurs **lately**. He had read **stack**s of books

---

★ **T. rex** (= Tyrannosaurus rex) 티라노사우루스 렉스. '폭군 도마뱀'이라는 뜻으로, 지구상에 살았던 육식 공룡 중 가장 무섭고 사나운 공룡으로 알려져 있다.

✱ **Triceratops** 트리케라톱스. '세 개의 뿔이 있는 얼굴'이라는 뜻으로, 입 끝이 새의 부리 모양이고 눈과 콧등 위에 뿔이 세 개 있는 초식 공룡.

from the library and had watched every dinosaur movie from the video store.

And today he had come specially **prepared**. Unlike the others, who were wearing their **regular** clothes, he had **dress**ed very carefully.

"Isn't that hat hot?" Arthur asked.

Buster shook his head. "It's not a hat—it's a pith helmet.★ This is what **paleontologist**s wear. It keeps them cool under the hot **desert** sun."

Arthur looked around. "Um, Buster, maybe you haven't **notice**d, but we're not in the desert."

Buster **shrug**ged. "Well, I **burn easily**. And it's better to be ready for anything. **Expect** the unexpected, that's my **motto**." He **pat**ted his **utility** belt. "Which is why we brought along all these **tool**s."

"Don't **remind** me," said Arthur, **shift**ing

★ **pith helmet** 피스 헬멧. 햇볕으로부터 머리를 보호하기 위해 쓰는 가볍고 단단한 소재로 된 흰색 모자.

his heavy **backpack**.

"You'll thank me later. We don't want to **be caught unprepared**. Hey, where did we put the chisels?*"

"I've got them," said Arthur.

"What about the field guides?*"

"Got those, too."

"Oooh! I hope we didn't forget—"

"Don't worry," said Arthur, patting his side pocket. "I have the **brush**es right here."

Mr. Ratburn called for everyone's **attention**. "Excuse me, children. If you could please quiet down."

Some of the class turned toward him, but a few of the kids continued **growl**ing at one another.

"QUIET!" Mr. Ratburn shouted.

★ chisel 끌. 나무, 돌, 금속 등에 구멍을 뚫거나 깎아내기 위한 공구.
* field guide 식물이나 조류에 대한 휴대용 도감.

The growling stopped.

"Thank you," Mr. Ratburn said **calm**ly. "As you know, we've come to the park today to learn more about dinosaurs and the **evidence** of their **existence** long ago."

He **stare**d for a moment at Binky and Francine. "All dinosaurs and students need to be on their best behavior. Is that clear?"

Francine **nod**ded. Binky just looked at the ground.

"Excellent," said Mr. Ratburn. "Now follow me, and we'll get started."

Chapter

2

Mr. Ratburn **led** the way through the **entrance** into a small museum. In the first room there were some glass **case**s **display**ing bones and rocks. Along one wall was a diorama★ showing a brachiosaurus✲ and a hadrosaurus✳ eating in a **swamp**.

"I'd get tired of eating nothing but salad all day," said Francine.

★ diorama 디오라마. 여러 모형을 배경과 함께 설치하여 특정 장면을 구성한 전시품.

✲ brachiosaurus 브라키오사우루스. '팔 도마뱀'이라는 뜻으로, 앞다리가 뒷다리보다 훨씬 긴 거대한 초식 공룡.

✳ hadrosaurus 하드로사우루스. '하돈필드의 도마뱀'이란 뜻으로, 미국 뉴저지주의 하돈필드에서 처음 발견된 초식 공룡.

Muffy agreed. "Even with the finest **import**ed **dressing**, it would get pretty **boring**."

Mr. Ratburn had approached a park **ranger** who **appear**ed to be waiting for him. They **shook hands** and **exchange**d hellos.

"Class, this is Ranger Ruth," Mr. Ratburn **announce**d. "She's going to tell us a few things about **fossil**s before we go out and **explore** for ourselves."

Ranger Ruth smiled sweetly at the class. "Hi, kids! Gosh, don't you look like a smart **bunch** of boys and girls! Can any of you tell me what a fossil is?"

A few kids **roll**ed **their eyes**.

Buster **raise**d his hand.

"Oh, good. A **volunteer**. Now, don't be shy. What do you think a fossil is?"

Buster took a deep **breath**. "Fossils are the **calcified remain**s of **ancient organism**s. **Mineral**s **seep** into these organisms' **tissue**s and **harden**,

preserving their **original form**s."

"Well, well, well!" Ranger Ruth looked **stun**ned. "**Count on** me to pick out the class **genius**. Moving right along, we have a little show for you to see. LIGHTS!"

As the lights **dim**med in the room, a **spotlight shine**d on the **dinosaur** diorama.

Ranger Ruth spoke into a **microphone**. "A hundred million years ago, Rainbow Rock **State** Park looked very different. It was much hotter. There were lots of **fern**s."

At that moment, a park ranger **dress**ed as a fern **shuffle**d into view.

"There were also lots of **insect**s," Ranger Ruth continued.

Another ranger, dressed as a **dragonfly, flap**ped onto the **stage**.

"Ewwww!" said the class together.

"And, of course, there were dinosaurs."

The kids **cheer**ed.

13

Two park rangers in a brachiosaurus **costume** **stumble**d onto the stage.

"**Eventually**, the ferns and animals died."

The fern costume **slump**ed to the floor.

The kids **giggle**d.

Then the dragonfly **collapse**d, and the brachiosaurus **split** apart, the front end remaining on the stage while the back end **ran off**.

Everyone laughed.

"Quiet, please!" said Mr. Ratburn.

"Thank you," said Ranger Ruth. "Now, usually the bodies would **rot** away. But once in a while, the hard parts of the bodies, like **shell**s and bones, would **last**."

The front part of the brachiosaurus un**zip**ped his costume, **reveal**ing a brachiosaurus **skeleton** costume underneath.

"Much much later, this whole area was **cover**ed by the sea. Over millions of years, the **soil** turned to rock. And the bones and shells

turned to rock, too."

The light **fade**d as the sound of **crash**ing **wave**s came over the **loudspeaker**s.

"Then the sea dried up. And finally, after another hundred million years, we're up to the **present**."

A spotlight was **switch**ed **on**, revealing a giant brachiosaurus skeleton on the far side of the **hall**.

The kids **applaud**ed as the lights came back on.

"Now," said Ranger Ruth, "who wants to **go on** a fossil hunt?"

Chapter

3

The class **hike**d behind **Ranger** Ruth through a **valley rim**med with high shale★ **cliff**s. Everyone was carrying a **pail** and **shovel**.

"I'm so excited!" Buster told Arthur.

"Really? I never would have guessed."

"I can't wait to **get my hands on** one of those fossils," Buster **went on**. "I mean, it's the real thing. The actual **impress**ion of something that was alive millions of years ago."

"Your **attention**, please!" said Ranger Ruth.

★ shale 셰일. 호수, 저수지, 늪지, 유속이 느리거나 거의 정지 상태에 있는 하천 등에서 퇴적된 진흙이 암석화된 퇴적암.

"Listen up!"

The class had stopped in front of one of the cliffs. The **layer**s of **dirt** and rock made different-colored **stripe**s in the cliff wall.

"You see the layers in this rock?" Ranger Ruth continued. "Each layer was **form**ed at a different time. The ones on the **bottom** are from the beginning of the Cretaceous **period**,★ around 135 million years ago."

"Wow," said Binky, "that was even before TV."

"Now, the top layers are from about twenty million years later," the ranger continued. "So we can tell how old a fossil is by **noting** where it was found in the cliff."

Muffy looked **confuse**d. "How will we get fossils out of the cliff?" she asked. "All we have are these little **bucket**s."

★ **Cretaceous period** 백악기. 중생대를 셋으로 나눈 것 중 마지막 시기. 약 1억 3,500만 년 전부터 6,500만 년 전까지의 기간을 말한다.

"Don't worry," said Ranger Ruth. "The cliffs are for the **professional paleontologist**s. You kids will hunt in the **stream**."

"In the stream?" said Francine. "Great!"

She **rush**ed into the water and began **splash**ing around.

"The water's great," she shouted. "Hey, look, I found a fossil! Oh, no, wait. It's a rock. Hey, here's another one!"

All of the children soon followed in after her.

Mr. Ratburn walked around, giving words of **encourage**ment. When he **reach**ed Arthur and Buster, he stopped to watch. Buster was **bob**bing up and down, **frantic**ally searching for fossils.

"Found anything yet, boys?"

"Noooooo!" they answered together.

"Oh. Well, we're going to **break** for a **snack** now, and then we'll be **head**ing back to the bus."

Arthur **straighten**ed up. "Well," he said, **stretch**ing, "I guess that's that."

"I'm not stopping till the very last minute," said Buster.

Arthur looked over at Mr. Ratburn and the ranger. They were getting out juice and cookies from an ice **chest**.★

"Buster! I see food! And drink!"

"I don't care," said Buster. "We can have snacks anytime. There are fossils here!"

"Are you sure you're feeling okay, Buster? I've never seen you **turn down** food before."

"Yes, I'm okay. I'm more than okay."

"**Come on**, then," said Arthur. "What do you **expect** to find in just a few more minutes? You're not going to just reach in and find something!"

Arthur reached his hand **underwater** and pulled up a stone with some **marking**s on it.

★ ice chest 아이스 박스. 얼음과 함께 음식을 넣어 냉장할 수 있도록 만든 냉장용기.

Buster turned to him angrily. Then his **expression** went **blank** when he saw what Arthur had in his hand.

"Buster? Are you okay?"

Buster began **advancing** slowly toward him. His hands were **outstretched**.

Arthur backed away. "Buster? Quit it! You're making me **nervous**."

Arthur **drop**ped the stone.

"Aaaaahhhhh!" said Buster.

He **dove** at the **spot** where the special stone fell in and began picking up any stone he could find. He **glance**d at each one, then threw it away.

"Buster, have you gone **nuts**?"

Buster picked up another stone, almost threw it away, too, and then **clutch**ed it to his chest.

"I found it! I found it!"

Arthur came over to see. "Found what?" he asked. "Show me."

Buster did. The stone showed an **imprint** with a three-**prong**ed **indent**ation.

"Oh, wow," said Arthur. "It's a leaf fossil."

"A leaf fossil? What do you mean, a leaf fossil? Have you even seen a leaf that thick?"

Buster held it up to the light. He took a deep **breath**. "Arthur," he **declared**, "*this* is a **footprint**."

Chapter 4

As the other kids ate their **snack**s, Buster sat with one hand **clench**ed on his pocket.

"Do you want a cookie, Buster?" Arthur asked.

Buster shook his head.

"How about some juice?"

Buster shook his head again. He was too excited to eat or drink. He was having enough trouble just **breathing**. **Imagine**! He had found a real **dinosaur fossil**. He could see the newspaper **headline**s now: BUSTER BAXTER'S BIG BREAK. Paleontologists from around the world would **line up** just to shake his hand.

Ranger Ruth **brush**ed a few cookie **crumb**s off her shirt. "I think everyone **work**ed **up** quite an **appetite**," she said. "While you finish up, let's go around and talk about the fossils we found."

Alex and the Brain held up a gray rock with **groove**s **spread**ing from the center.

"We think this might have been a **shell**," said the Brain.

Ranger Ruth took the rock and **examine**d it. "Very nice. And not just any shell. It looks like Emarginula.★"

She placed it in a box.

Alex and the Brain looked **pleased**. "Do you think it will **end up** on **display**?" the Brain asked.

"We'll see," said the ranger. "A lot of people

★ **Emarginula** 삿갓조개. 바위 지역에서 고둥과 함께 바위에 붙어 살며 눈에 잘 띄지 않는 조개로 타원형의 삿갓 모양이다.

beside myself are part of that decision."

Buster **blink**ed. "Wait a minute!" he cried. "Can't we all keep what we found?"

Ranger Ruth shook her head. "Oh, I'm sorry. Maybe you weren't listening when I explained earlier. We put as many fossils as we can in the museum so everyone can have a chance to see them."

"And you **include proper credit**," said the Brain.

"**Absolute**ly," said the ranger. "We always give credit to whoever finds our fossils."

She smiled at Buster. "Okay?"

"I guess." Buster sat down again. "I can't believe it," he **mutter**ed to himself. "How can they do this to me?"

Francine held up some rocks. "**Take a look** at these. I don't think there are any fossils here. But the rocks are still pretty interesting."

The ranger examined them. "Yes, they are.

Streaks of mica⋆ and quartz,✳ I believe. I think I'll **hold on to** them for **further** study."

Francine **beam**ed. "See that," she said to Muffy. "Further study. I found important rocks."

Muffy **shrug**ged. "The only really important rocks are the kind in rings and necklaces."

"Anyone else?" said Ranger Ruth.

A few more kids showed her what they had found.

Arthur **poke**d Buster in the side.

"Stop that!" **whisper**ed Buster.

"But . . . but . . . ," began Arthur.

"Do you boys have something to add?" the ranger asked. "Did our **budding expert** find anything he'd like to share?"

"Nothing," said Buster. "Nothing at all."

Arthur looked surprised. "What do you mean?"

★ mica 운모. 화강암 중 규산염 광물의 하나.

✳ quartz 석영. 지구상의 광물 중 두 번째로 흔한 광물로 유리, 도자기 등의 재료로 사용된다.

he whispered. "I thought we—"

Buster **elbow**ed Arthur in the **rib**s. "It's okay," he told Ranger Ruth. "Arthur's a little **embarrass**ed because we don't have anything to show you."

The ranger **pat**ted Arthur on the back. "Don't worry about it, Arthur. As scientists, we must learn **patience**. I'm sure you'll find something another time."

"I guess so," said Arthur, **glancing dark**ly at Buster. "I feel better already."

Chapter 5

There was still a little time for the kids to play before they had to leave. Binky went back to being a *T. rex,* **growl**ing and **claw**ing at everyone who passed by. Francine and Muffy **swoop**ed over the grass as pterodactyls★ looking for something to eat.

Arthur wasn't in the **mood** to play dinosaur. He was **nervous**.

"We're never going to **get away with** this," he told Buster quietly as they sat at a picnic

---

★ **pterodactyl** (= pterodactylus) 익룡. '날개의 발가락'이란 뜻으로, 트라이아스기 후기에서부터 백악기까지 살았던 하늘을 나는 파충류.

table.*

"We'll see," said Buster.

"But the fossil isn't ours—I mean, yours. I mean, you should get **credit** for finding it, but it **belong**s in the museum."

"I'm not **giving** it **up**," said Buster. He **squeeze**d the fossil gently. "It's like holding a **piece** of **history**."

"But what if they search us on the way out? We could get **arrest**ed! What if they have some special fossil-**detector alarm**?"

"I've never heard of such a thing."

"Well, that doesn't make me feel better," said Arthur. "Remember, the time Muffy brought goat cheese to class and you **insist**ed it was **fake**—because you had never heard of it?"

"That was different," said Buster. "It doesn't **make sense** that goats can make cheese if all

---

★ picnic table 야외에 설치된 간이테이블.

they eat are **tin** cans."

"Well, you found out differently, didn't you? And what about that *Bionic Bunny* episode where the scientist **invent**s an X-ray* laser? They could have one of those here."

Arthur looked around nervously.

"But *The Bionic Bunny* is a TV show," said Buster.

"I know. A lot of it is very **realistic**, though. **Base**d on true stories, I think."

"Maybe so," said Buster, "but I don't think—"

Tweeeeeeet!

Mr. Ratburn was **blow**ing his **whistle**.

"All right, everyone," he shouted, "let's **gather** around. The bus is here. Check your **belonging**s to make sure you don't leave anything behind."

Buster put his hand back on his pocket. The fossil was safe. His finger could feel the **rough**

★ **X-ray** X선. 빠르게 가속시킨 전자를 금속에 충돌시켰을 때 생기는 파장이 짧은 전자기파로, 뢴트겐 선이라고도 한다.

outline of the **footprint**.

"Uh-oh," said Arthur. "Look, Buster, **Ranger** Ruth is coming toward us. She's going to **frisk** us. I told you this would happen. But did you want to listen? Noooooo. They must have some kind of detector hidden in the trees. It's probably **trigger**ed by an infrared—*"

"Sssssh!" **hiss**ed Buster.

Ranger Ruth came right up to Buster and stopped.

"Any last thing you want to ask me?" she said.

"Um, I don't think so."

The ranger laughed. "Well, perhaps there's something you want to tell me instead."

"What kind of thing?"

"Well, I'm not sure. It could be some new dinosaur fact. Or maybe . . ."

Arthur squeezed his eyes shut. It was coming.

★ **infrared** 적외선. 가시광선 범위의 한 끝인 적색 스펙트럼을 벗어난 비가시광선.

The gamma-ray* **detection net** had caught them for sure. They were **goner**s.

". . . you might want to tell me you had a good time."

Buster **brighten**ed **at once**. "Oh, yes."

"You look a little un**comfortable**," said the ranger. She **pat**ted Buster on the back. "I hope you're not too **discourage**d about your fossil hunting. You **have the makings of** a real **paleontologist**."

"Thanks."

She went off to say good-bye to Mr. Ratburn.

"See?" said Buster. "We're perfectly safe."

"Maybe for now," said Arthur.

★ **gamma-ray** 감마선. 방사성 원소에서 나오는 방사선 가운데 하나로 파장이 극히 짧고 물질 투과성이 강한 전자기파이다.

Chapter

6

After school, Arthur wanted to tell Francine and the Brain about the **fossil**, but Buster wouldn't allow it.

"Too dangerous," he explained.

"Well, who *can* we tell?" Arthur asked.

"Nobody. We have to keep it a secret."

When Buster got home, he went straight to his room. He closed the door and pulled down his window **shade**.

"**Perimeter security in place**," he said.

Next, he **wrap**ped the fossil in **tinfoil**. Then he put it inside a plastic bag and put the bag in a shoe box.

"**Phase** One complete."

He **fill**ed the **rest** of the shoe box with **marble**s from a **bowl** and put it on a **shelf** in his **closet**.

"Phase Two complete," he said. "Security protocol★ **set. Alert status confirm**ed."

At dinner with his mother and grandmother, Buster didn't say much.

"Are you feeling okay?" his mother asked. "You're **awful**ly quiet."

"Just tired, I guess," said Buster.

"How did the field **trip** go?"

"Okay," said Buster.

"Did you find any nice fossils?"

Buster almost **knock**ed over his milk.

"Fossils? What makes you ask that?"

"I don't know, Buster. I thought that's why

★ protocol 프로토콜. 원래는 국가간의 교류를 원활하게 하는 외교상의 의례나 국가 간의 약속을 정한 의정서를 말하지만, 여기서는 보안을 위한 절차라는 뜻으로 사용되었다.

you went to the park."

"Oh, right. Well, it was pretty interesting. There was a show. The ranger was **friendly**. And then we got to walk around."

His mother **nod**ded. "I'm glad you enjoyed yourself."

"When I was your age," said Buster's grandmother, "we didn't go fossil hunting." She **pause**d. "Back then, **dinosaur**s were still alive, of course."

Buster's mother laughed.

Buster just **roll**ed **his eyes**.

"What's that you've done to your **mash**ed potatoes?*" his mother asked.

Buster looked down at his **plate**.

"It kind of looks like a dinosaur footprint," his mother **went on**.

"No, no," said Buster, **scoop**ing up a **bite** and

★ mashed potato 삶은 감자를 으깬 뒤 버터와 우유를 섞어서 만드는 요리.

swallowing it. "Just a **design**. That's all."

A little later, Buster went up to his room for the night. He **toss**ed **and turn**ed a long time before he finally fell asleep.

Thummmp! Thummp!

"What's that noise?" Buster **wonder***ed. He looked out his window.*

A large dinosaur was looking back at him.

"There you are!" said the dinosaur.

"Who, me?" said Buster.

"Yes, you—the boy who took my footprint. I want it back—now!"

"I think you're **confusing** *me with somebody else," said Buster.*

"No, I'm not," said the dinosaur. "Maybe you think you can **ignore** *me because I'm not that big. Don't be* **fool***ed. I have big and powerful friends."*

The dinosaur **flick***ed his tail behind him. Buster saw a tyrannosaurus and a triceratops standing there. The tyrannosaurus, though, had*

Binky's head, and the triceratops had Francine's.

"Give back the footprint!" they shouted.

"Never!" said Buster, and he **slam**med the window shut.

What was he going to do? What were they going to do?

Suddenly the room began to shake. His books **tumble**d off their shelves, and a box of colored pencils **spill**ed onto the floor.

"We're coming!" said the voices outside. "We want the footprint!"

Buster **grab**bed the shoe box with the fossil in it and held it tightly.

The room **tremble**d around him, and he waited for the end to come.

Chapter 7

"Wow!" said Arthur. "That was some dream."

He and Buster were sitting at their desks before class started the next morning. Buster had been **relating** the **detail**s of his **nightmare**.

"The worst part," said Buster, "was that Binky's head looked so natural on top of the tyrannosaurus."

"What about Francine's?"

Buster laughed. He looked at Francine, who was talking with Muffy and Sue Ellen on the other side of the room. "She never looks completely normal," he said.

Arthur nodded. He was happy Buster had told him about the dream, but he was even happier he hadn't dreamed it himself.

"At least it's over," said Buster.

"True," said Arthur. "But don't you think your dream was trying to tell you something?"

Buster **consider**ed it.

"Yes, it was telling me not to put so much chocolate **sauce** on my apple pie. I think I got a little **stomachache** before **bedtime**."

Arthur **sigh**ed. "So when can I **come over** and see it?"

"You can't. No one can."

Arthur looked surprised. "Why not?"

"I've made very careful **security arrangement**s. They should not be **disturb**ed."

"I'll be careful," Arthur **insist**ed.

"Sorry. It's too dangerous. What if my mom came in?"

"But Buster, what's the **point** of having the

you-know-what★ if we can't even look at it?"

Buster was saved from trying to answer that question because Francine was on her way over.

"Good morning, Arthur. You look kind of tired, Buster. Didn't sleep well, huh? Probably feeling bad because you didn't find anything yesterday."

"What do you mean?"

"I mean at the park. You're the big **expert**, Mr. **Paleontologist**."

Buster's face got red. "It's true that I like fossils."

"And yet with all your **knowledge**, all your **tool**s . . . and, yes, let's not forget your hat—"

"Pith helmet," Buster corrected her.

"Pith helmet," Francine repeated. "Even with all that, you didn't find anything."

★ you-know-what 말할 수 없거나 말하고 싶지 않은 대상을 가리킬 때 이름을 대신해서 사용하는 표현.

Buster was silent.

"You're not being **fair**, Francine," said Arthur. "Buster did a good job looking yesterday." Arthur **stare**d hard at Francine. "A really good job."

She just laughed.

"Excuse me," said Mr. Ratburn. "Let's take our places."

When the whole class was seated, he continued.

"I hope you all enjoyed our field **trip** yesterday. I know it was exciting to have the chance to find a real fossil. Of course, finding them isn't easy. It would have been **amazing** if we had found **sign**s of any dinosaur bones or teeth."

Arthur **fidget**ed a little while Buster put his hands over his mouth and **cover**ed his eyes with his long ears.

"Or, even **rare**r, dinosaur **footprint**s. Wouldn't that have been exciting?"

Everyone nodded.

Mr. Ratburn **shrug**ged. "But this time it didn't happen. What's that, Buster?"

"Nothing, Mr. Ratburn."

"Oh. I thought I heard you **groan**. Well, anyway, just remember that **throughout history** the great scientists have met with **disappoint**ment first and then **triumph**ed later on."

Buster **slump**ed forward on his desk. Keeping this secret was getting to be a lot harder than he had thought.

Chapter

8

Mrs. Baxter was worried.

"Are you okay, honey?" she asked.

Buster jumped off his bed. "Okay? Of course, I'm okay. Why wouldn't I be okay? Don't I look okay?"

His mother wasn't so sure. "Well, you look a little tired. You're not having any problems at school, are you?"

"No, no," said Buster, "everything at school is fine."

The phone rang.

Buster ran to answer it.

"Hello?"

"Hi," said Arthur. "I had a question about our math homework. **Are** we **supposed to measure** things by the *foot*★ or the *meter?*✳"

"*Foot?* What makes you say *foot?*"

"How else should I say it?" Arthur asked.

"You don't **fool** me," said Buster. "You know perfectly well we're supposed to do both. You're just **check**ing **up on** my *you-know-what.*"

"**Honestly**, Buster, I couldn't remember if—"

"Yeah, yeah. Nice try, Arthur. I'll see you tomorrow. Bye."

He **hung up** the phone and returned to his room.

He found his mother holding the shoe box.

"What's this, Buster? It feels kind of heavy."

"That?" Buster **rush**ed over and took it out of

★ **foot** 길이의 단위 피트(feet). 1피트는 30.48센티미터이다.
✳ **meter** 길이의 단위인 미터. 1미터는 100센티미터이다.

her hand. "It's a school **project**. Very **delicate**. **Hush-hush**. **Top secret**. Can't talk about it now."

He put it back in the **closet**.

His mother looked **concern**ed. "You need some **rest**, honey. Maybe you should go to bed early."

Buster **glance**d at the window. "Bed? Early?" he **squeak**ed. "Sounds good."

Sometime later, Buster lay in bed, thinking about **fossil**s. His **eyelid**s began to **droop**.

*There was a **knock** at the door.*

"Who is it?" asked Buster.

"Fossil Police."

"Huh?" said Buster.

*The door **burst** open. **Ranger** Ruth and a police officer entered. They were **drag**ging Arthur behind them. He was wearing a **striped prisoner**'s **uniform**.*

*"I'm sorry, Buster," said Arthur. "They made me tell. They **tickle**d me."*

"Why didn't you **defend** yourself?" Buster asked.

Arthur held up his arms. He was wearing **handcuff**s.

"Not a pretty picture, is it?" said Ranger Ruth. "And we've got the same **treat**ment ready for you."

"Me?" said Buster. "What did I do?"

The ranger laughed. "We have reason to believe you're hiding a **dinosaur** in this room."

Buster's eyes **dart**ed to his closet. "But that's **ridiculous**! There haven't been any dinosaurs for millions of years. How could—"

Ranger Ruth and the officer followed Buster's **gaze** to his closet. Then they **halt**ed, hearing a **strange** sound.

Tromp, tromp, tromp.

"Care to explain that, Mr. Paleontologist?" asked Ranger Ruth.

"Explain what?" said Buster. "I don't hear

51

anything."

TROMP, TROMP, TROMP.

*"Stand back," said the ranger. "We're **about to**—"*

Suddenly the closet door burst open. A Tyrannosaurus rex *stepped out, **roaring** at them.*

*"**Guilty** as **charged**," said the ranger.*

"He looks hungry," said Arthur.

*"Don't worry," said the ranger. "We're perfectly safe. He's only mad at Buster for keeping him **cooped up** in the closet."*

The tyrannosaurus opened his mouth wide, showing every one of his teeth.

Buster screamed.

Buster was **absent** from school the next day. Arthur wasn't really worried because he **figure**d that Buster was just sick. But he decided to go by the Baxters' apartment on his way home.

Mrs. Baxter let him in.

"Hello, Arthur, how are you?"

"Fine."

Mrs. Baxter **sigh**ed. "I wish I could say the same for Buster. I kept him home today because he didn't sleep well last night. I don't think he's sick or **contagious**, though, so you can go see him."

"Thanks, Mrs. Baxter."

When Arthur **reach**ed Buster's room, he found the door closed. He **knock**ed.

"Buster! It's me, Arthur."

Buster opened the door. He was still wearing his **pajamas**.

"You're **just in time**, Arthur. I need help with the final **preparation**s."

Arthur **blink**ed. The room was a **mess**. Everything had been emptied out of the **closet**, and there was a **web** of **string crisscross**ing the room.

"What are you doing?" Arthur asked.

"Well, first I emptied my closet. That way I can tell what's inside with a quick look. I don't want any dinosaurs hiding in there." He **point**ed to the string. "And now I'm making a dinosaur **detector**. When the dinosaurs come, they're not going to catch me by surprise."

"But Buster, dinosaurs have been **extinct**

for millions of years. You know that."

"I think that's just what they want us to believe. It's all part of their **master plan**."

"Their master plan?"

Buster **nod**ded. "That's why they've left all those fossils to find. They want to **trick** us. But I'm not **fool**ed. I'm going to be ready."

Arthur sat down on the bed.

"Don't you think you're **go**ing a little **overboard**?"

Buster **snort**ed. "You wouldn't say that if you'd had the dream I had last night. Actually, you were there. Not the real you, of course, but the dream you. It was pretty **scary**."

He took out a shoe box from under the bed.

"Here," said Buster. "You take this."

"Why?"

"The fossil's inside. You said you wanted to see it before. Now you can have it."

"Buster, I don't want the fossil, either. It isn't right."

Buster **rub**bed his eyes. "I have to **get rid of** it, Arthur. I'm going crazy."

Arthur took another look around the room. "So I see," he said.

"I thought it would be so great, having this million-year-old thing to myself. I thought I would feel special and important. But all I feel is . . ."

"Guilty?"

Buster **pace**d **back and forth**. "I don't know. But it's driving me **nuts**, that's for sure. I can't even look at it anymore."

Arthur **stare**d at the box. "The fossil doesn't **belong** here or at my house," he said. "You know that."

Buster sighed. "So where *does* it belong?"

Arthur **gave** him **a look**. *"You* tell *me,"* he said.

Chapter

10

Inside the Rainbow Rock Visitor Center, Arthur and Buster were **anxious**ly standing by the door.

"They're taking a long time," said Buster. He **rub**bed his hands together. "Maybe we shouldn't have come."

Arthur tried to smile. "Now, don't start *that* again. . . ."

Buster **paced back and forth**. "I can't help it," he said. "I'm not good at waiting. Do you think there's a problem?"

"I sure hope not," said Arthur.

Finally, **Ranger** Ruth approached them. One of the **staff paleontologist**s was with her.

"Good afternoon, boys," she said. "I'm glad to see you again."

"And we're glad to be here," said Arthur. He looked **nervous**ly at Buster. "Aren't we?"

Buster **nod**ded. "So, what can you tell us?" he asked excitedly.

Ranger Ruth **fold**ed her arms. "No decision has been made."

Arthur **sigh**ed.

"Basically, we're just not sure yet," said the paleontologist.

"Still?" said Buster. It had been a whole month since he and Arthur had returned the **fossil** to Ranger Ruth. They had surprised her, both because the fossil was **rare** and because Buster had taken it from the park **in the first place**. But she was **please**d that he had returned it. And when she heard about his **nightmare**s, she decided to **go easy on** him.

The paleontologist smiled. "I understand how you feel, Buster. **Unfortunately**, these things take time. We have to do a spectral **analysis**,★ carbon-14 dating . . .*"

"I know, I know," said Buster. "Science can't be **rush**ed. But I was hoping for a decision before *I* become a fossil."

"We're getting closer," said the paleontologist. "Dr. Marsh thinks your fossil is the **footprint** of a baby daspletosaurus.* Dr. Cope, however, thinks it's an adult coelosaur.*"

"And what do you think?" asked Arthur.

"I think it's great that you two found the

★ **spectral analysis** 스펙트럼분석법. 외부에너지의 자극을 받고 나온 빛의 스펙트럼을 분해하여 광물에 존재하는 원소를 측정하는 방법.

✻ **carbon-14 dating** 방사선 탄소 연대 측정법. 유물이나 유적의 내부에 잔존하는 방사성 탄소의 농도를 측정하여 그 물체의 제작 시점을 측정하는 방법.

✻ **daspletosaurus** 다스플레토사우루스. '무서운 도마뱀'이란 뜻으로, 백악기 후기에 살았던 육식 공룡.

✻ **coelosaur** 코엘루로사우르. 앞다리가 길고 몸집이 작은 공룡으로 조류의 시조로 추측된다.

fossil in the first place."

Buster **beam**ed. "It did take a lot of looking." He stopped to think. "The **odds** were against us. Luckily, we had brought our **tool**s. The pith helmet especially helped a lot. I could see the fossil clearly when Arthur held it up. I might have missed it **otherwise**."

"Speaking of not missing things," said Ranger Ruth, "I want to show you something."

She walked them over to the **display case**.

Next to the fossil footprint was a **brass plaque**. It read *Dinosaur* Footprint, *Discover*ed by Buster Baxter and Arthur Read.

"Wow!" said Buster. "Our very own **nameplate**."

"I've never seen my name look so **fancy**," said Arthur.

"I think it's gold," said Buster. He **pause**d. "But how long does it get to stay there?"

"For as long as the fossil **last**s," said Ranger Ruth.

Buster smiled. "That's long enough for me," he said.

버스터의
공룡 대소동

CONTENTS

대한민국 영어 학습자라면 꼭 한번 읽어봐야 할, 아서 챕터북 시리즈!

아서 챕터북 시리즈(Arthur Chapter Book series)는 미국의 작가 마크 브라운(Marc Brown)이 쓴 책입니다. 레이크우드 초등학교에 다니는 주인공 아서(Arthur)가 소소한 일상에서 벌이는 다양한 에피소드를 담은 이 책은, 기본적으로 미국 초등학생들을 위해 쓰인 책이지만 누구나 공감할 만한 재미있는 스토리로 출간된 지 30년이 넘은 지금까지 남녀노소 모두에게 큰 사랑을 받고 있습니다. 아서가 주인공으로 등장하는 이야기는 리더스북과 챕터북 등 다양한 형태로 출판되었는데, 현재 미국에서만 누적 판매 부수가 6천6백만 부를 돌파한 상황으로 대한민국 인구 숫자보다 더 많은 책이 판매된 것을 생각하면 그 인기가 어느 정도 인지 실감할 수 있습니다.

특히 이 『아서 챕터북』은 한국에서 영어 학습자를 위한 최적의 원서로 큰 사랑을 받고 있기도 합니다. 『영어 낭독 훈련』, 『잠수네 영어 학습법』, 『솔빛이네 엄마표 영어연수』 등 많은 영어 학습법 책들에서 『아서 챕터북』을 추천 도서로 선정하고 있으며, 수많은 영어 고수들과 영어 선생님들, '엄마표 영어'를 진행하는 부모님들에게도 반드시 거쳐 가야 하는 영어원서로 전폭적인 지지를 얻고 있습니다.

번역과 단어장이 포함된 워크북, 그리고 오디오북까지 담긴 풀 패키지!

이 책은 이렇게 큰 사랑을 받고 있는 영어원서 『아서 챕터북』 시리즈에, 더욱 탁월한 학습 효과를 거둘 수 있도록 다양한 콘텐츠를 덧붙인 책입니다.
• 영어원서: 본문에 나온 어려운 어휘에 볼드 처리가 되어 있어 단어를 더욱 분명히 인지하며 자연스럽게 암기하게 됩니다.
• 단어장: 원서에 나온 어려운 어휘가 '한영'은 물론 '영영' 의미까지 완벽하게 정리되어 있으며, 반복되는 단어까지 넣어두어 자연스럽게 복습이 되도록 구성했습니다.
• 번역: 영어와 비교할 수 있도록 직역에 가까운 번역을 담았습니다. 원서 읽기에 익숙하지 않은 초보 학습자들도 어려움 없이 내용을 파악할 수 있습니다.
• 퀴즈: 현직 원어민 교사가 만든 이해력 점검 퀴즈가 들어있습니다.
• 오디오북: 미국 현지에서 판매중인 빠른 속도의 오디오북(분당 약 145단어)과

국내에서 녹음된 따라 읽기용 오디오북(분당 약 110단어)을 포함하고 있어 듣기 훈련은 물론 소리 내어 읽기에까지 폭넓게 사용할 수 있습니다.

이 책의 수준과 타깃 독자

- 미국 원어민 기준: 유치원 ~ 초등학교 저학년
- 한국 학습자 기준: 초등학교 저학년 ~ 중학교 1학년
- 영어원서 완독 경험이 없는 초보 영어 학습자 (토익 기준 450~750점대)
- 비슷한 수준의 다른 챕터북: Magic Tree House, Marvin Redpost, Zack Files, Captain Underpants
- 도서 분량: 5,000단어 초반 (약 5,000~5,200단어)

아서 챕터북, 이렇게 읽어보세요!

- **단어 암기는 이렇게!** 처음 리딩을 시작하기 전, 해당 챕터에 나오는 단어들을 눈으로 쭉 훑어봅니다. 모르는 단어는 좀 더 주의 깊게 보되, 손으로 써가면서 완벽하게 암기할 필요는 없습니다. 본문을 읽으면서 이 단어들을 다시 만나게 되는데, 그 과정에서 단어의 쓰임새와 어감을 자연스럽게 익히게 됩니다. 이렇게 책을 읽은 후에, 단어를 다시 한번 복습하세요. 복습할 때는 중요하다고 생각하는 단어들을 손으로 써가면서 꼼꼼하게 외우는 것도 좋습니다. 이런 방식으로 책을 읽다보면, 많은 단어를 빠르고 부담 없이 익히게 됩니다.

- **리딩할 때는 리딩에만 집중하자!** 원서를 읽는 중간 중간 모르는 단어가 나온다고 워크북을 들춰보거나, 곧바로 번역을 찾아보는 것은 매우 좋지 않은 습관입니다. 모르는 단어나 이해가 가지 않는 문장이 나온다고 해도 펜으로 가볍게 표시만 해두고, 전체적인 맥락을 잡아가며 빠르게 읽어나가세요. 리딩을 할 때는 속도에 대한 긴장감을 잃지 않으면서 리딩에만 집중하는 것이 좋습니다. 모르는 단어와 문장은, 리딩이 끝난 후에 한꺼번에 정리해보는 '리뷰'시간을 갖습니다. 리뷰를 할 때는 번역은 물론 단어장과 사전도 꼼꼼하게 확인하면서 왜 이해가 되지 않았는지 확인해 봅니다.

- **번역 활용은 이렇게!** 이해가 가지 않는 문장은 번역을 통해서 그 의미를 파악할

수 있습니다. 하지만 한국어와 영어는 정확히 1:1 대응이 되지 않기 때문에 번역을 활용하는 데에도 지혜가 필요합니다. 의역이 된 부분까지 억지로 의미를 대응해서 암기하려고 하기보다, 어떻게 그런 의미가 만들어진 것인지 추측하면서 번역은 참고자료로 활용하는 것이 좋습니다.

● **듣기 훈련은 이렇게!** 리스닝 실력을 향상시키길 원한다면 오디오북을 적극적으로 활용하세요. 처음에는 오디오북을 틀어놓고 눈으로 해당 내용을 따라 읽으면서 훈련을 하고, 이것이 익숙해지면 오디오북만 틀어놓고 '귀를 통해' 책을 읽어보세요. 눈으로는 한 번도 읽지 않은 책을 귀를 통해 완벽하게 이해할 수 있다면 이후에는 영어 듣기로 고생하는 일은 거의 없을 것입니다.

● **소리 내어 읽고 녹음하자!** 이 책은 특히 소리 내어 읽기(Voice Reading)에 최적화된 문장 길이와 구조를 가지고 있습니다. 또한 오디오북 CD에 포함된 '따라 읽기용' 오디오북으로 소리 내어 읽기 훈련을 함께할 수 있습니다. 소리 내어 읽기를 하면서 내가 읽은 것을 녹음하고 들어보세요! 자신의 영어 발음을 들어보는 것은 몹시 민망한 일이지만, 그 과정을 통해서 의식적 · 무의식적으로 발음을 교정하게 됩니다. 이렇게 영어로 소리를 만들어 본 경험은 이후 탄탄한 스피킹 실력의 밑거름이 될 것입니다.

● **2~3번 반복해서 읽자!** 영어 초보자라면 2~3회 반복해서 읽을 것을 추천합니다. 초보자일수록 처음 읽을 때는 생소한 단어들과 스토리 때문에 내용 파악에 급급할 수밖에 없습니다. 하지만 일단 내용을 파악한 후에 다시 읽으면 어휘와 문장 구조 등 다른 부분까지 관찰하면서 조금 더 깊이 있게 읽을 수 있고, 그 과정에서 리딩 속도도 빨라지고 리딩 실력을 더 확고하게 다지게 됩니다.

● **'시리즈'로 꾸준히 읽자!** 한 작가의 책을 시리즈로 읽는 것 또한 영어 실력 향상에 큰 도움이 됩니다. 같은 등장인물이 다시 나오기 때문에 내용 파악이 더 수월할 뿐 아니라, 작가가 사용하는 어휘와 표현들도 자연스럽게 반복되기 때문에 탁월한 복습 효과까지 얻을 수 있습니다. 『아서 챕터북』 시리즈는 현재 10권, 총 50,000단어 분량이 출간되어 있습니다. 이 책들을 시리즈로 꾸준히 읽으면서 영어 실력을 쑥쑥 향상시켜 보세요!

영어원서 본문 구성

내용이 담긴 본문입니다.
원어민이 읽는 일반 원서와 같은 텍스트지만, 암기해야 할 중요 어휘들은 볼드체로 표시되어 있습니다. 이 어휘들은 지금 들고 계신 워크북에 챕터별로 정리되어 있습니다.

학습 심리학 연구 결과에 따르면, 한 단어씩 따로 외우는 단어 암기는 거의 효과가 없다고 합니다. 대신 단어를 제대로 외우기 위해서는 문맥(Context) 속에서 단어를 암기해야 하며, 한 단어 당 문맥 속에서 15번 이상 마주칠 때 완벽하게 암기할 수 있다고 합니다.

이 책의 본문은 중요 어휘를 볼드로 강조하여, 문맥 속의 단어들을 더 확실히 인지(Word Cognition in Context)하도록 돕고 있습니다. 또한 대부분의 중요한 단어들은 다른 챕터에서도 반복해서 등장하기 때문에 이 책을 읽는 것만으로도 자연스럽게 어휘력을 향상시킬 수 있습니다.

또한 본문에는 내용 이해를 돕기 위해 '각주'가 첨가되어 있습니다. 각주는 굳이 암기할 필요는 없지만, 알아두면 내용을 더 깊이 있게 이해할 수 있어 원서를 읽는 재미가 배가됩니다.

워크북(Workbook)의 구성

Check Your Reading Speed
해당 챕터의 단어 수가 기록되어 있어, 리딩 속도를 측정할 수 있습니다. 특히 리딩 속도를 중시하는 독자들이 유용하게 사용할 수 있습니다.

Build Your Vocabulary
본문에 볼드 표시되어 있는 단어들이 정리되어 있습니다. 리딩 전, 후에 반복해서 보면 원서를 더욱 쉽게 읽을 수 있고, 어휘력도 빠르게 향상됩니다.

단어는 〈빈도 – 스펠링 – 발음기호 – 품사 – 한글 뜻 – 영문 뜻〉 순서로 표기되어 있으며 빈도 표시(★)가 많을수록 필수 어휘입니다. 반복 등장하는 단어는 빈도 대신 '복습'으로 표기되어 있습니다. 품사는 아래와 같이 표기했습니다.

n. 명사 ｜ a. 형용사 ｜ ad. 부사 ｜ v. 동사 ｜ conj. 접속사 ｜ prep. 전치사 ｜ int. 감탄사
idiom 숙어 및 관용구

Comprehension Quiz
간단한 퀴즈를 통해 읽은 내용에 대한 이해력을 점검해 볼 수 있습니다.

번역
영문과 비교할 수 있도록 최대한 직역에 가까운 번역을 담았습니다.

오디오북 CD 구성

이 책은 '듣기 훈련'과 '소리 내어 읽기 훈련'을
위한 2가지 종류의 오디오북이 포함되어 있습
니다.
- 듣기 훈련용 오디오북: 분당 145단어 속도
  (미국 현지 판매 중인 오디오북)
- 소리 내어 읽기 훈련용 오디오북: 분당 110
  단어 속도

오디오북은 MP3 파일로 제공되는 MP3 기기나
컴퓨터에 옮겨서 사용하셔야 합니다. 오디오북
에 이상이 있을 경우 helper@longtailbooks.co.kr로 메일을 주시면 자세한 안내를
받으실 수 있습니다.

EBS 동영상 강의 안내

EBS의 어학사이트(EBSlang.co.kr)에서 『아서 챕터북』 동영상 강의가 진행되고 있습니다.
영어 어순의 원리에 맞게 빠르고 정확하게 이해하는 법을 완벽하게 코치해주는 국내 유일의 강의!
저렴한 수강료에 완강 시 50% 환급까지!
지금 바로 열광적인 수강 평가와 샘플 강의를 확인하세요!
http://www.EBSreading.com

Chapter 1

1. **Where was Mr. Ratburn's third grade class headed on a field trip?**
   A. Rocky Mountain State Park
   B. Rainbow Rock State Park
   C. Ratburn Falls State Park
   D. Rolling Stones State Park

2. **What was a great thing to do at the place they went?**
   A. Hunt for fossils of ancient animals
   B. See wildlife in their natural habitat
   C. Go swimming in the river
   D. Work of school reports

3. How did Binky and Francine act after getting off the bus?

A. They pretended to be sick in order to go home.

B. They pretended to be tour guides for the field trip.

C. They started to bully Arthur and Buster.

D. They pretended to be dinosaurs.

4. How did Buster come dressed to the field trip?

A. He came dressed like a paleontologist.

B. He came dressed like a professor.

C. He came dressed like a doctor.

D. He came dressed like a dinosaur.

5. Which of the following was something that Buster did NOT ask Arthur if he brought?

A. Field guides

B. Chisels

C. Gloves

D. Brushes

$$\frac{461 \ words}{reading \ time \ (\quad) \ sec} \times 60 = (\quad\quad) \ WPM$$

Build Your Vocabulary

- **rest** [rest] n. 나머지 (사람들·것들); 휴식; v. 쉬다; 기대다
  The rest is used to refer to all the parts of something or all the things in a group that remain or that you have not already mentioned.

- **cheer** [ʧiər] v. 환호성을 지르다; 힘을 북돋우다; n. 환호(성)
  When people cheer, they shout loudly to show their approval or to encourage someone who is doing something such as taking part in a game.

- **ride** [raid] v. (차량·자전거·말 등을) 타다; n. (차량·자전거 등을) 타고 달리기; 여정; 승마
  When you ride a bicycle or a motorcycle, you sit on it, control it, and travel along on it.

- **state** [steit] n. 주(州); 국가, 나라; 상태; v. 말하다, 진술하다; 명시하다
  (state park n. 주립공원)
  Some large countries such as the USA are divided into smaller areas called states.

- **trip** [trip] n. 여행; 발을 헛디딤; v. 발을 헛디디다; ~를 넘어뜨리다 (field trip n. 현장 학습)
  A trip is a journey that you make to a particular place.

- **fossil** [fásəl] n. 화석
  A fossil is the hard remains of a prehistoric animal or plant that are found inside a rock.

ancient [éinʃənt] a. 고대의; 아주 오래된
Ancient means belonging to the distant past, especially to the period in history before the end of the Roman Empire.

include [inklúːd] v. 포함하다, 포함시키다
If one thing includes another thing, it has the other thing as one of its parts.

dinosaur [dáinəsɔːr] n. 공룡
Dinosaurs were large reptiles which lived in prehistoric times.

pull to a stop idiom 서다, 멈추다
When a driver or vehicle pulls to a stop or a halt, the vehicle stops.

exit [égzit] v. 나가다, 떠나다; 퇴장하다; n. 출구
If you exit from a room or building, you leave it.

line up idiom 줄을 서다
If people line up, they form a line, standing one behind the other or beside each other.

orderly [ɔ́ːrdərli] a. (행동이) 질서 있는; 정돈된
If something is done in an orderly fashion or manner, it is done in a well-organized and controlled way.

fashion [fǽʃən] n. 방법, 방식; 유행; v. 만들다, 빚다
If you do something in a particular fashion or after a particular fashion, you do it in that way.

pile [pail] v. (많은 사람들이) 우르르 가다; 쌓다, 포개다; n. 쌓아 놓은 것; 더미, 무더기
If a group of people pile into or out of a vehicle, they all get into it or out of it in a disorganized way.

leap [liːp] v. (leapt-leapt) 뛰다, 뛰어넘다; (서둘러) ~하다; n. 높이뛰기, 도약; 급증, 급등
If you leap somewhere, you move there suddenly and quickly.

pavement [péivmənt] n. 포장 도로, 인도
A pavement is a path with a hard surface, usually by the side of a road.

claw [klɔ:] v. (손톱·발톱으로) 할퀴다; n. (동물의) 발톱; 갈고리
If an animal claws at something, it scratches or damages it with its claws.

stamp [stæmp] v. (발을) 구르다; (도장 등을) 찍다; n. 우표; 도장
If you stamp or stamp your foot, you lift your foot and put it down very hard on the ground.

fierce [fiərs] a. 사나운, 험악한; 격렬한, 맹렬한
A fierce animal or person is very aggressive or angry.

beast [bi:st] n. (특히 덩치가 크고 위험한) 짐승, 야수
You can refer to an animal as a beast, especially if it is a large, dangerous, or unusual one.

count [kaunt] v. (수를) 세다; 계산하다; 포함시키다; n. 셈, 계산; 수치
When you count, you say all the numbers one after another up to a particular number.

lately [léitli] ad. 최근에, 얼마 전에
You use lately to describe events in the recent past, or situations that started a short time ago.

stack [stæk] n. 무더기, 더미; v. 쌓다, 포개다; 채우다
A stack of things is a pile of them.

prepare [pripέər] v. 준비하다; 대비하다, 각오하다 (prepared a. 준비가 되어 있는)
If you prepare for an event or action that will happen soon, you get yourself ready for it or make the necessary arrangements.

regular [régjulər] a. 보통의, 평상시의; 규칙적인; n. 단골손님
Regular is used to mean 'normal.'

dress [dres] v. (특정한 유형의) 옷차림을 하다; 옷을 입다; n. 드레스; 옷
If someone dresses in a particular way, they wear clothes of a particular style or color.

paleontologist [peiliəntálədʒist] n. 고생물학자
A paleontologist is a specialist in paleontology which is the earth science that studies fossil organisms and related remains.

desert [dézərt] ① n. 사막; a. 불모의 ② v. 버리다; 떠나다
A desert is a large area of land, usually in a hot region, where there is almost no water, rain, trees, or plants.

notice [nóutis] v. ~을 의식하다; 주목하다; n. 주목; 안내문
If you notice something or someone, you become aware of them.

shrug [ʃrʌg] v. (어깨를) 으쓱하다; n. (어깨를) 으쓱하기
If you shrug, you raise your shoulders to show that you are not interested in something or that you do not know or care about something.

burn [bə:rn] v. (햇볕 등에) 타다; 태우다; n. 화상
If you burn or get burned in the sun, the sun makes your skin become red and sore.

easily [í:zili] ad. 쉽게, 잘; 수월하게, 용이하게
You use easily to say that something happens more quickly or more often than is usual or normal.

expect [ikspékt] v. 예상하다, 기대하다; 요구하다 (**unexpected** a. 예기치 않은, 예상 밖의)
If you expect something to happen, you believe that it will happen.

motto [mátou] n. 좌우명, 모토
A motto is a short sentence or phrase that expresses a rule for sensible behavior, especially a way of behaving in a particular situation.

pat [pæt] v. 쓰다듬다, 토닥거리다; n. 쓰다듬기
If you pat something or someone, you tap them lightly, usually with your hand held flat.

utility [ju:tíləti] a. 다용도의, 다목적의; n. 유용성
You use utility to describe something useful, especially through being able to perform several functions.

tool [tu:l] n. 도구, 연장; 수단
A tool is any instrument or simple piece of equipment that you hold in your hands and use to do a particular kind of work.

remind [rimáind] v. 상기시키다, 다시 한 번 알려 주다
If someone reminds you of a fact or event that you already know about, they say something which makes you think about it.

shift [ʃift] v. 이동하다, 옮기다; (견해·태도·방식을) 바꾸다; n. 변화
If you shift something or if it shifts, it moves slightly.

backpack [bǽkpæk] n. 배낭
A backpack is a bag with straps that go over your shoulders, so that you can carry things on your back when you are walking or climbing.

be caught unprepared idiom 허를 찔리다
If you are caught unprepared for something, you are not ready for it, and you are therefore surprised or at a disadvantage when it happens.

brush [brʌʃ] n. 솔; 붓; 빗자루; v. 솔질을 하다; (솔이나 손으로) 털다
A brush is an object which has a large number of bristles or hairs fixed to it.

attention [əténʃən] n. 주의, 주목; 관심
If you give someone or something your attention, you look at it, listen to it, or think about it carefully.

growl [graul] v. 으르렁거리다; 으르렁거리듯 말하다; n. 으르렁거리는 소리
When a dog or other animal growls, it makes a low noise in its throat, usually because it is angry.

calm [kaːm] a. 침착한, 차분한; 잔잔한; v. 진정시키다; n. 평온; 진정
(calmly ad. 침착하게, 태연하게)
You can use calmly to emphasize that someone is behaving in a very controlled or ordinary way in a frightening or unusual situation.

evidence [évədəns] n. 증거, 흔적; v. 증거가 되다, 증언하다
Evidence is anything that you see, experience, read, or are told that causes you to believe that something is true or has really happened.

existence [igzístəns] n. 존재, 실재, 현존
The existence of something is the fact that it is present in the world as a real thing.

* **stare** [stɛər] v. 빤히 쳐다보다, 응시하다; n. 빤히 쳐다보기, 응시
If you stare at someone or something, you look at them for a long time.

⁑ **nod** [nad] v. (고개를) 끄덕이다, 끄덕여 나타내다; n. (고개를) 끄덕임
If you nod, you move your head downward and upward to show agreement, understanding, or approval.

Chapter

2

1. What did Buster volunteer to do?

A. He volunteered to describe different kinds of dinosaurs.

B. He volunteered to ask the class to quiet down.

C. He volunteered to explain how to find fossils.

D. He volunteered to explain how fossils formed.

2. What did Ranger Ruth show the students?

A. A video about fossils in museums

B. A poster presentation about fossils

C. A play on a stage about fossils

D. Her private fossil collection

3. What part of the show caused the students to laugh?

A. A ranger dressed like dinosaur splitting apart

B. A ranger dressed like a tree falling down

C. A ranger dressed like a dragonfly

D. A ranger tripping over a fossil

4. Which of the following was NOT how the area had looked millions of years ago?

A. It had once been covered by the sea.

B. It had once had a lot of ferns.

C. It had once had dinosaurs.

D. It had once had a volcano.

5. What was revealed at the end of the show?

A. The cliffs where the students would hunt for fossils

B. The special written report for the field trip

C. A giant brachiosaurus skeleton

D. A giant tyrannosaurus skeleton

$$\frac{506 \text{ words}}{\text{reading time (\quad) sec}} \times 60 = (\quad) \text{ WPM}$$

Build Your Vocabulary

lead [liːd] ① v. (led–led) 이끌다; 지휘하다; 선두를 달리다; n. 선두, 우세 ② n. [광물] 납
If you lead a group of people, you walk or ride in front of them.

entrance [éntrəns] n. 입구, 문; 입장, 등장
The entrance to a place is the way into it, for example a door or gate.

case [keis] n. 용기, 통, 상자; 사례, 경우; 사건
A case is a container that is specially designed to hold or protect something.

display [displéi] v. 전시하다, 진열하다; 드러내다; n. 전시, 진열
If you display something that you want people to see, you put it in a particular place, so that people can see it easily.

swamp [swamp] n. 늪, 습지; v. 쇄도하다, 넘쳐 나다
A swamp is an area of very wet land with wild plants growing in it.

import [impɔ́ːrt] v. 수입하다; n. 수입품; 수입
To import products or raw materials means to buy them from another country for use in your own country.

dressing [drésiŋ] n. (요리용) 드레싱, 소스
A salad dressing is a mixture of oil, vinegar, and herbs or flavorings, which you pour over salad.

boring [bɔ́ːriŋ] a. 재미없는, 지루한
Someone or something boring is so dull and uninteresting that they make people tired and impatient.

ranger [réindʒər] n. 삼림 관리원
A ranger is a person whose job is to look after a forest or large park.

appear [əpíər] v. ~인 것 같다; 나타나다, 보이기 시작하다
If you say that something appears to be the way you describe it, you are reporting what you believe or what you have been told, though you cannot be sure it is true.

shake hands idiom 악수하다
If you shake hands with someone, you take their right hand in your own for a few moments, often moving it up and down slightly, when you are saying hello or goodbye to them, congratulating them, or agreeing on something.

exchange [ikstʃéindʒ] v. 교환하다, 주고받다; n. 교환; 대화
If two or more people exchange things of a particular kind, they give them to each other at the same time.

announce [ənáuns] v. 발표하다, 알리다; 단언하다
If you announce something, you tell people about it publicly or officially.

fossil [fásəl] n. 화석
A fossil is the hard remains of a prehistoric animal or plant that are found inside a rock.

explore [iksplɔ́ːr] v. 답사하다, 탐사하다; 탐구하다
If you explore a place, you travel around it to find out what it is like.

bunch [bʌntʃ] n. (한 무리의) 사람들; 다발, 송이; v. 단단해지다; 단단히 접히다
A bunch of people is a group of people who share one or more characteristics or who are doing something together.

roll one's eyes idiom 눈을 굴리다
If you roll your eyes, they move round and upward when they are frightened, bored, or annoyed.

raise [reiz] v. 들어올리다, 들다; 불러일으키다, 자아내다
If you raise something, you move it so that it is in a higher position.

volunteer [vàləntíər] n. 자원해서 하는 사람; 자원 봉사자; v. 자원하다
A volunteer is someone who offers to do a particular task or job without being forced to do it.

breath {breθ} n. 숨, 입김 (take a deep breath idiom 심호흡하다)
When you take a deep breath, you breathe in a lot of air at one time.

calcify [kǽlsəfài] v. 석회화하다
To calcify something means to become hard or make something hard, especially by the addition of substances containing calcium.

remain [riméin] n. (pl.) 유해; 유적; 나머지; v. 계속 ~이다; 남아 있다
The remains of a person or animal are the parts of their body that are left after they have died.

ancient [éinʃənt] a. 고대의; 아주 오래된
Ancient means belonging to the distant past, especially to the period in history before the end of the Roman Empire.

organism [ɔ́:rgənìzm] n. 생물(체), 유기체
An organism is an animal or plant, especially one that is so small that you cannot see it without using a microscope.

mineral [mínərəl] n. 광물(질); 무기물
A mineral is a substance such as tin, salt, or sulphur that is formed naturally in rocks and in the earth.

seep [si:p] v. 스미다, 배다
If something such as liquid or gas seeps somewhere, it flows slowly and in small amounts into a place where it should not go.

tissue [tíʃu:] n. (pl.) (세포) 조직; 화장지
In animals and plants, tissue consists of cells that are similar to each other in appearance and that have the same function.

harden [haːrdn] v. 굳다, 경화되다; (감정·태도가) 단호해지다
When something hardens or when you harden it, it becomes stiff or firm.

preserve [prizə́ːrv] v. 보존하다; 지키다, 보호하다; n. 전유물
If you preserve something, you take action to save it or protect it from damage or decay.

original [ərídʒənl] a. 원래의, 본래의; 독창적인; n. 원본
You use original when referring to something that existed at the beginning of a process or activity, or the characteristics that something had when it began or was made.

form [fɔːrm] n. 모습, 형체; 종류; 방식; v. 형성되다, 구성하다
The form of something is its shape.

stun [stʌn] v. 놀라게 하다, 아연하게 하다; 기절시키다 (stunned a. 어리벙벙한)
If you are stunned by something, you are extremely shocked or surprised by it and are therefore unable to speak or do anything.

count on idiom ~을 믿다; ~을 확신하다
If you count on someone or something, you rely on someone to do something or expect something to happen and make plans in an appropriate way.

genius [dʒíːnjəs] n. 천재; 천재성; 특별한 재능
A genius is a highly talented, creative, or intelligent person.

dim [dim] v. 어둑해지다; (감정·특성이) 약해지다; a. 어둑한, 흐릿한; (눈이) 침침한
If you dim a light or if it dims, it becomes less bright.

spotlight [spátlàit] n. 스포트라이트, 조명; 주목, 관심; v. 집중 조명하다
A spotlight is a powerful light, for example in a theater, which can be directed so that it lights up a small area.

shine [ʃain] v. 빛나다, 반짝이다; 비추다; n. 윤기; 광택
When the sun or a light shines, it gives out bright light.

dinosaur [dáinəsɔːr] n. 공룡
Dinosaurs were large reptiles which lived in prehistoric times.

microphone [máikrəfòun] n. 마이크(로폰)
A microphone is a device that is used to make sounds louder or to record them on a tape recorder.

state [steit] n. 주(州); 국가, 나라; 상태; v. 말하다; 진술하다; 명시하다
(state park n. 주립공원)
Some large countries such as the USA are divided into smaller areas called states.

fern [fəːrn] n. [식물] 양치식물
A fern is a plant that has long stems with feathery leaves and no flowers.

dress [dres] v. (특정한 유형의) 옷차림을 하다; 옷을 입다; n. 드레스; 옷
If someone dresses in a particular way, they wear clothes of a particular style or color.

shuffle [ʃʌfl] v. 발을 끌며 걷다; (카드를) 섞다; n. 발을 끌며 걷기; (카드를) 섞기
If you shuffle somewhere, you walk there without lifting your feet properly off the ground.

insect [ínsekt] n. 곤충, 벌레
An insect is a small animal that has six legs. Most insects have wings. Ants, flies, butterflies, and beetles are all insects.

dragonfly [drǽgənflai] n. [곤충] 잠자리
Dragonflies are brightly-colored insects with long, thin bodies and two sets of wings. Dragonflies are often found near slow-moving water.

flap [flæp] v. 퍼덕거리다; 펄럭거리다; n. (봉투·호주머니 등에 달린) 덮개; 펄럭거림
If a bird or insect flaps its wings or if its wings flap, the wings move quickly up and down.

stage [steidʒ] n. 무대; 단계; v. (연극·공연 등을) 개최하다; (일을) 벌이다
In a theater, the stage is an area where actors or other entertainers perform.

cheer [ʧiər] v. 환호성을 지르다; 힘을 북돋우다; n. 환호(성)
When people cheer, they shout loudly to show their approval or to encourage someone who is doing something such as taking part in a game.

costume [kástjuːm] n. 분장, 변장; 의상, 복장
An actor's costume is the set of clothes they wear while they are performing.

stumble [stʌmbl] v. 비틀거리다; 발을 헛디디다; 더듬거리다
If you stumble, you put your foot down awkwardly while you are walking or running and nearly fall over.

eventually [ivénʧuəli] ad. 결국, 마침내
Eventually means at the end of a situation or process or as the final result of it.

slump [slʌmp] v. 털썩 앉다; 급감하다, 급락하다; n. 급감, 폭락; 불황
If you slump somewhere, you fall or sit down there heavily, for example because you are very tired or you feel ill.

giggle [gigl] v. 피식 웃다, 킥킥거리다; n. 피식 웃음, 킥킥거림
If someone giggles, they laugh in a childlike way, because they are amused, nervous, or embarrassed.

collapse [kəlǽps] v. 쓰러지다; 주저앉다; 붕괴되다; n. 붕괴, 실패; 쓰러짐
If you collapse, you suddenly faint or fall down because you are very ill or weak.

split [split] v. (split-split) 찢다, 쪼개다; 나누다; 분열되다; n. (길게 찢어진) 틈; 분할
If something splits or if you split it, it is divided into two or more parts.

run off idiom (~에서) 달아나다, 도망치다
To run off means to move quickly away from someone or a place.

rot [rat] v. 썩다, 부패하다; n. 썩음, 부패
When food, wood, or another substance rots, or when something rots it, it becomes softer and is gradually destroyed.

shell [ʃel] n. (달걀 · 견과류 등의) 껍데기; 뼈대; v. 껍질을 까다
The shell of an animal such as a tortoise, snail, or crab is the hard protective covering that it has around its body or on its back.

last [læst] v. 오래가다, 지속되다; 계속되다; a. 최후의; 지난
If something lasts for a particular length of time, it continues to be able to be used for that time, for example because there is some of it left or because it is in good enough condition.

zip [zip] v. 지퍼로 잠그다; 쌩 하고 가다; n. 지퍼 (unzip v. 지퍼를 열다)
When you unzip something which is fastened by a zip or when it unzips, you open it by pulling open the zip.

reveal [rivíːl] v. (보이지 않던 것을) 드러내 보이다; (비밀 등을) 밝히다
If you reveal something that has been out of sight, you uncover it so that people can see it.

skeleton [skélətn] n. 뼈대, 골격; 해골
Your skeleton is the framework of bones in your body.

cover [kʌ́vər] v. 덮다; 씌우다, 가리다; n. (책이나 잡지의) 표지; 덮개
If one thing covers another, it forms a layer over its surface.

soil [sɔil] n. 토양, 흙; v. 더럽히다
Soil is the substance on the surface of the earth in which plants grow.

fade [feid] v. 서서히 사라지다; 바래다, 희미해지다
When light fades, it slowly becomes less bright.

crash [kræʃ] v. 부딪치다; 충돌하다; 굉음을 내다; n. 요란한 소리; (자동차 · 항공기) 사고
If something crashes somewhere, it moves and hits something else violently, making a loud noise.

wave [weiv] n. 파도, 물결; (팔 · 손 · 몸을) 흔들기; v. 흔들다; 손짓하다
A wave is a raised mass of water on the surface of water, especially the sea, which is caused by the wind or by tides making the surface of the water rise and fall.

loudspeaker [láudspìːkər] n. 확성기, 스피커
A loudspeaker is a piece of equipment, for example part of a radio or hi-fi system, through which sound comes out.

present [préznt] ① n. 현재; a. 현재의; 참석한 ② v. 소개하다; 주다, 수여하다; n. 선물
The present is the period of time that we are in now and the things that are happening now.

switch on idiom (전등 등의) 스위치를 켜다
If you switch on something like an electrical device, a machine, or an engine, you start them by pressing a switch or a button.

hall [hɔːl] n. 넓은 방, 홀; (건물 안의) 복도; 현관
A hall is a large room or building which is used for public events such as concerts, exhibitions, and meetings.

applaud [əplɔ́ːd] v. 박수를 치다; 갈채를 보내다
When a group of people applaud, they clap their hands in order to show approval, for example when they have enjoyed a play or concert.

go on idiom 시작하다; 말을 계속하다; (어떤 상황이) 계속 되다
When you go on something, you start doing a particular activity or being in a particular state.

Chapter

3

1. **How could Ranger Ruth tell how old a fossil was in the cliff?**
   A. By the color of the fossil
   B. By the kind of animal it used to be
   C. By where it was found in the layers of the cliff
   D. By the plants that grew around the animal fossils

2. **Where did Ranger Ruth tell the class to hunt for fossils?**
   A. On the sides of the cliff wall
   B. In the stream
   C. In the museum
   D. In the desert

3. Why did Mr. Ratburn's class take a break from fossil hunting?

A. Nobody was finding any fossils.

B. Buster had broken a fossil.

C. It was too hot outside to work.

D. They were going to eat a snack.

4. Why did Arthur ask if Buster was feeling okay?

A. He had never seen him turn down food before.

B. He had never seen him so excited about school before.

C. He had never seen him so focused on a field trip before.

D. He had never seen him ignore a teacher before.

5. What did Arthur think the fossil that they found might have been?

A. A footprint

B. A leaf

C. A fork

D. A foot

Check Your Reading Speed
1분에 몇 단어를 읽는지 리딩 속도를 측정해보세요.

$$\frac{614 \text{ words}}{\text{reading time ( ) sec}} \times 60 = (\quad) \text{ WPM}$$

Build Your Vocabulary

hike [haik] v. 하이킹을 가다; n. 하이킹
If you hike, you go for a long walk in the country.

ranger [réindʒər] n. 삼림 관리원
A ranger is a person whose job is to look after a forest or large park.

valley [væli] n. 골짜기, 계곡
A valley is a low stretch of land between hills, especially one that has a river flowing through it.

rim [rim] v. 가장자리를 두르다; n. (둥근 물건의) 가장자리, 테두리 (rimmed a. 테를 두른)
If something is rimmed with a substance or color, it has that substance or color around its border.

cliff [klif] n. 절벽, 낭떠러지
A cliff is a high area of land with a very steep side, especially one next to the sea.

pail [peil] n. 들통, 양동이
A pail is a bucket, usually made of metal or wood.

shovel [ʃʌvəl] n. 삽; v. 삽질하다, 삽으로 파다
A shovel is a tool with a long handle that is used for lifting and moving earth, coal, or snow.

get one's hands on idiom (필요한 것을) 손에 넣다; 붙잡아 혼내주다
If you get your hands on something, you manage to find it or obtain it, usually after some difficulty.

go on idiom 말을 계속하다; (어떤 상황이) 계속되다; 시작하다
When you go on, you continue speaking after a short pause.

impress [imprés] v. 새기다; 깊은 인상을 주다, 감명을 주다 (impression n. 자국; 인상)
An impression of an object is a mark or outline that it has left after being pressed hard onto a surface.

attention [əténʃən] n. 주의, 주목; 관심
If you give someone or something your attention, you look at it, listen to it, or think about it carefully.

layer [léiər] n. 층, 막; v. 층층이 놓다
A layer of a material or substance is a quantity or piece of it that covers a surface or that is between two other things.

dirt [dəːrt] n. 흙; 먼지, 때
You can refer to the earth on the ground as dirt, especially when it is dusty.

stripe [straip] n. 줄무늬
A stripe is a long line which is a different color from the areas next to it.

form [fɔːrm] v. 형성되다, 구성하다; n. 모습, 형체; 종류; 방식
When something natural forms or is formed, it begins to exist and develop.

bottom [bátəm] n. 맨 아래, 뒷면; 바닥; a. 맨 아래쪽에
The bottom of something is the lowest or deepest part of it.

period [píːəriəd] n. 기간, 시기; 마침표
A particular length of time in history is sometimes called a period.

note [nout] v. ~에 주목하다; 언급하다; n. 메모; 쪽지
If you note a fact, you become aware of it.

confuse [kənfjúːz] v. (사람을) 혼란시키다; 혼동하다 (confused a. 혼란스러워 하는)
If you are confused, you do not know exactly what is happening or what to do.

bucket [bʌ́kit] n. 양동이, 들통; 한 양동이(의 양)
A bucket is a round metal or plastic container with a handle attached to its sides.

professional [prəféʃənl] a. 전문가의; 전문적인; 능숙한; n. 전문직 종사자
Professional people have jobs that require advanced education or training.

paleontologist [peiliəntάlədʒist] n. 고생물학자
A paleontologist is a specialist in paleontology which is the earth science that studies fossil organisms and related remains.

stream [striːm] n. 개울, 시내; (액체·기체의) 줄기; v. 줄줄 흐르다; 줄을 지어 이어지다
A stream is a small narrow river.

rush [rʌʃ] v. 급히 움직이다, 서두르다; 재촉하다; n. 혼잡, 분주함; (감정이) 치밀어 오름
If you rush somewhere, you go there quickly.

splash [splæʃ] v. 첨벙거리다; (물·흙탕물 등을) 끼얹다; n. 첨벙 하는 소리; 방울
If you splash about or splash around in water, you hit or disturb the water in a noisy way, causing some of it to fly up into the air.

encourage [inkɔ́ːridʒ] v. 격려하다, 용기를 북돋우다; 권장하다
(encouragement n. 격려(가 되는 것))
If you encourage someone, you give them confidence, for example by letting them know that what they are doing is good and telling them that they should continue to do it.

reach [riːʧ] v. 이르다, 도달하다; (손·팔을) 뻗다, 내밀다; n. 거리; 범위
When someone or something reaches a place, they arrive there.

bob [bab] v. (급하게) 위아래로 움직이다; (고개를) 까닥거리다; n. (머리·몸을) 까닥거림
If something bobs, it moves up and down, like something does when it is floating on water.

frantic [fræntik] a. 정신없이 하는; 제정신이 아닌 (frantically ad. 미친 듯이)
If an activity is frantic, things are done quickly and in an energetic but disorganized way, because there is very little time.

break [breik] v. 쉬다, 휴식하다; 깨다, 부수다; (법·약속 등을) 어기다; n. 휴식; 운수
If someone breaks for a short period of time, they rest or change from what they are doing for a short period.

snack [snæk] n. 간식, 간단한 식사; v. 간식을 먹다
A snack is a simple meal that is quick to cook and to eat.

head [hed] v. (특정 방향으로) 향하다; ~을 이끌다; n. 머리, 고개; 책임자
If you are heading for a particular place, you are going toward that place.

straighten [streitn] v. (자세를) 바로 하다; 똑바르게 되다
If you straighten up from a bent position, you make your back or body straight and upright.

stretch [stretʃ] v. 기지개를 켜다; 잡아 늘이다; n. (길게) 뻗은 지역; (계속되는) 기간
When you stretch, you put your arms or legs out straight and tighten your muscles.

chest [tʃest] ① n. 상자, 궤 (ice chest n. 아이스박스) ② n. 가슴, 흉부
An ice chest is a chilled box for keeping something cold, especially food.

turn down idiom ~을 거절하다, 거부하다
If you turn someone or something down, you reject or refuse them.

come on idiom 서둘러, 빨리; 자 어때
You use 'come on' to encourage someone do something, for example, to hurry.

expect [ikspékt] v. 예상하다, 기대하다; 요구하다
If you expect something to happen, you believe that it will happen.

underwater [ʌndərwɔ́:tər] ad. 물속에서, 수면하에; a. 물속의, 수중의
Something that exists or happens underwater exists or happens below the surface of the sea, a river, or a lake.

marking [máːrkiŋ] n. (pl.) 무늬, 반점; 표시
Markings are colored lines, shapes, or patterns on the surface of something, which help to identify it.

expression [ikspréʃən] n. 표정; 표현, 표출
Your expression is the way that your face looks at a particular moment. It shows what you are thinking or feeling.

blank [blæŋk] a. 멍한, 무표정한; 빈; n. 빈칸, 여백; v. (갑자기) 멍해지다
If you look blank, your face shows no feeling, understanding, or interest.

advance [ædvǽns] v. 다가가다, 진격하다; 증진되다; n. 전진; 진전, 발전
To advance means to move forward, often in order to attack someone.

outstretched [àutstréʧt] a. 쭉 뻗은, 펼친
If a part of the body of a person or animal is outstretched, it is stretched out as far as possible.

nervous [nə́ːrvəs] a. 불안해하는, 초조해하는; 겁을 잘 먹는
If someone is nervous, they are frightened or worried about something that is happening or might happen, and show this in their behavior.

drop [drap] v. 떨어뜨리다; 약해지다, 낮추다; n. 방울; 하락, 감소
If you drop something, you accidentally let it fall.

dive [daiv] v. (dove/dived–dived) 휙 움직이다; (물 속으로) 뛰어들다; n. 다이빙, (물 속으로) 뛰어들기
If you dive in a particular direction or into a particular place, you jump or move there quickly.

spot [spat] n. 곳, 장소; (작은) 점; 얼룩; v. 발견하다, 찾다, 알아채다
You can refer to a particular place as a spot.

glance [glæns] v. 흘깃 보다; 대충 훑어보다; n. 흘깃 봄
If you glance at something or someone, you look at them very quickly and then look away again immediately.

nuts [nʌts] a. 미친, 제정신이 아닌
If you say that someone goes nuts or is nuts, you mean that they go crazy or are very foolish.

clutch [klʌtʃ] v. (꽉) 움켜잡다; n. 움켜쥠; (세력의) 손아귀
If you clutch at something or clutch something, you hold it tightly, usually because you are afraid or anxious.

imprint [ímprint] n. 자국; 각인; v. 각인시키다; 찍다, 새기다
An imprint is a mark or outline made by the pressure of one object on another.

prong [prɔːŋ] n. (뾰족하게 나뉘어져 있는) 갈래 (pronged a. 가닥이 진, 갈래진)
The prongs of something such as a fork are the long, thin pointed parts.

indent [indént] v. (각인·자국 등을) 찍다, 눌러 찍다; (글의 행을) 들여 쓰다; n. 오목한 곳 (indentation n. 자국)
An indentation is a shallow hole or cut in the surface or edge of something.

breath [breθ] n. 숨, 입김 (take a deep breath idiom 심호흡하다)
When you take a deep breath, you breathe in a lot of air at one time.

declare [diklέər] v. 언명하다, 분명히 말하다; 선언하다
If you declare that something is true, you say that it is true in a firm, deliberate way. You can also declare an attitude or intention.

footprint [fútprint] n. (사람·동물의) 발자국
A footprint is a mark in the shape of a foot that a person or animal makes in or on a surface.

Chapter

4

1. Why could Buster not eat or drink anything during their break?

A. He had a dentist appointment.

B. He was too excited.

C. He was feeling sick.

D. He was already full.

2. What did Ranger Ruth want the class to do while they finished their snacks?

A. She wanted them to talk about their favorite dinosaur fossils.

B. She wanted them to talk about the fossils that they had found.

C. She wanted them to talk about what they wanted to be in the future.

D. She wanted them to talk about the fossils that they wished they had found.

3. What happened to the fossils that were found in the area?

A. They were sent overseas for more research.

B. They were sent back to school with the students.

C. They were kept in the museum with proper credit.

D. They were given to whomever found them.

4. Why did Francine think the rocks she had found were important?

A. Because Ranger Ruth said she would hold on to them for further study.

B. Because Ranger Ruth said she had been searching for those for a long time.

C. Because Ranger Ruth said they were especially rare rocks.

D. Because Ranger Ruth let Francine keep them for herself.

5. How did Buster react to Ranger Ruth asking if he and Arthur had found anything?

A. He told her that they had found nothing.

B. He was excited to show her their fossil.

C. He was embarrassed that he had nothing to share.

D. He said that he would try harder next time.

1분에 몇 단어를 읽는지 리딩 속도를 측정해보세요.

$$\frac{514 \ words}{reading \ time \ (\quad) \ sec} \times 60 = (\quad) \ WPM$$

Build Your Vocabulary

snack [snæk] n. 간식, 간단한 식사; v. 간식을 먹다
A snack is a simple meal that is quick to cook and to eat.

clench [klentʃ] v. (주먹을) 꽉 쥐다; ~을 단단히 고정시키다
When you clench your fist or your fist clenches, you curl your fingers up tightly, usually because you are very angry.

breathe [briːð] v. 호흡하다, 숨을 쉬다
When people or animals breathe, they take air into their lungs and let it out again.

imagine [imǽdʒin] v. 상상하다, (마음속으로) 그리다
If you imagine something, you think about it and your mind forms a picture or idea of it.

dinosaur [dáinəsɔːr] n. 공룡
Dinosaurs were large reptiles which lived in prehistoric times.

fossil [fάsəl] n. 화석
A fossil is the hard remains of a prehistoric animal or plant that are found inside a rock.

headline [hédlain] n. (신문 기사의) 표제; (pl.) 주요 뉴스들; v. (기사에) 표제를 달다
A headline is the title of a newspaper story, printed in large letters at the top of the story, especially on the front page.

break [breik] n. 운수; 휴식; v. 쉬다, 휴식하다; 깨다, 부수다; (법·약속 등을) 어기다
(big break n. 큰 성공)
A break is a lucky opportunity that someone gets to achieve something.

line up idiom 줄을 서다
If people line up, they form a line, standing one behind the other or beside each other.

brush [brʌʃ] v. (솔이나 손으로) 털다; 솔질을 하다; n. 붓; 솔; 빗자루
If you brush something somewhere, you remove it with quick light movements of your hands.

crumb [krʌm] n. (빵·케이크의) 부스러기; 약간, 소량
Crumbs are tiny pieces that fall from bread, biscuits, or cake when you cut it or eat it.

work up idiom ~을 불러일으키다, ~을 북돋우다
If you work something up, you gradually develop or increase them until you have enough.

appetite [ǽpətàit] n. 식욕
Your appetite is your desire to eat.

groove [gruːv] n. 홈; (음악의) 리듬
A groove is a deep line cut into a surface.

spread [spred] v. 펼쳐지다; 펼치다; 확산시키다; n. 확산, 전파; 길이
If something such as a liquid, gas, or smoke spreads or is spread, it moves outwards in all directions so that it covers a larger area.

shell [ʃel] n. (달걀·견과류 등의) 껍데기; 뼈대; v. 껍질을 까다
The shell of an animal such as a tortoise, snail, or crab is the hard protective covering that it has around its body or on its back.

examine [igzǽmin] v. 조사하다, 검토하다; 검사하다, 진찰하다
If you examine something, you look at it carefully.

please [pliːz] v. 기쁘게 하다, 기분을 맞추다; ~하고 싶다; int. 부디, 제발
(pleased a. 기뻐하는, 만족해하는)
If you are pleased, you are happy about something or satisfied with something.

end up idiom (결국) ~하게 되다
If you end up doing something or end up in a particular state, you reach or come to a particular place or situation that you did not expect or intend to be in.

display [displéi] n. 전시, 진열; v. 전시하다, 진열하다; 드러내다
A display is an arrangement of things that have been put in a particular place, so that people can see them easily.

blink [bliŋk] v. 눈을 깜박이다; (불빛이) 깜박거리다; n. 눈을 깜박거림
When you blink or when you blink your eyes, you shut your eyes and very quickly open them again.

include [inklúːd] v. 포함하다, 포함시키다
If one thing includes another thing, it has the other thing as one of its parts.

proper [prάpər] a. 적절한, 제대로 된; 올바른, 정당한
The proper thing is the one that is correct or most suitable.

credit [krédit] n. 칭찬, 인정; 신용 거래; v. ~을 ~로 여기다; ~를 ~의 공으로 믿다
If you get the credit for something good, people praise you because you are responsible for it, or are thought to be responsible for it.

absolute [ǽbsəlùːt] a. 완전한, 완벽한; 확실한 (absolutely ad. 전적으로, 틀림없이)
Absolutely means totally and completely.

mutter [mʌ́tər] v. 중얼거리다; 투덜거리다; n. 중얼거림
If you mutter, you speak very quietly so that you cannot easily be heard, often because you are complaining about something.

take a look idiom ~을 한 번 보다
When you take a look at something, you look at it with attention.

streak [striːk] n. (바탕과 색깔이 다른) 기다란 줄무늬; v. 줄무늬를 넣다
A streak is a long stripe or mark on a surface which contrasts with the surface because it is a different color.

hold on to idiom 계속 보유하다; ~을 맡아 주다
If you hold on to something, you keep or do not lose them.

further [fɔ́ːrðər] a. 더 이상의, 추가의; ad. 더; 더 멀리에; v. 발전시키다
A further thing, number of things, or amount of something is an additional thing, number of things, or amount.

beam [biːm] v. 활짝 웃다; 비추다; n. 빛줄기; 환한 미소
If you say that someone is beaming, you mean that they have a big smile on their face because they are happy, pleased, or proud about something.

shrug [ʃrʌg] v. (어깨를) 으쓱하다; n. (어깨를) 으쓱하기
If you shrug, you raise your shoulders to show that you are not interested in something or that you do not know or care about something.

poke [pouk] v. (손가락 등으로) 쿡 찌르다; 쑥 내밀다; n. 찌르기
If you poke someone or something, you quickly push them with your finger or with a sharp object.

whisper [hwíspər] v. 속삭이다, 소곤거리다; n. 속삭임, 소곤거리는 소리
When you whisper, you say something very quietly.

budding [bʌ́diŋ] a. 신예의; 싹트기 시작하는
If you describe someone as, for example, a budding businessman or a budding artist, you mean that they are starting to succeed or become interested in business or art.

expert [ékspəːrt] n. 전문가; a. 전문가의, 전문적인; 숙련된
An expert is a person who is very skilled at doing something or who knows a lot about a particular subject.

elbow [élbou] v. (팔꿈치로) 밀치다; n. 팔꿈치
If you elbow people aside or elbow your way somewhere, you push people with your elbows in order to move somewhere.

rib [rib] n. 갈비(뼈), 늑골
Your ribs are the 12 pairs of curved bones that surround your chest.

embarrass [imbǽrəs] v. 당황스럽게 하다, 쑥스럽게 하다; 곤란하게 하다
(embarrassed a. 쑥스러운, 당황스러운)
A person who is embarrassed feels shy, ashamed, or guilty about something.

pat [pæt] v. 쓰다듬다, 토닥거리다; n. 쓰다듬기
If you pat something or someone, you tap them lightly, usually with your hand held flat.

patience [péiʃəns] n. 참을성, 인내심
If you have patience, you are able to stay calm and not get annoyed, for example when something takes a long time, or when someone is not doing what you want them to do.

glance [glæns] v. 흘낏 보다; 대충 훑어보다; n. 흘낏 봄
If you glance at something or someone, you look at them very quickly and then look away again immediately.

dark [daːrk] a. 사악한, 음흉한; 어두운, 캄캄한; 검은(색의); n. 어둠, 암흑
(darkly ad. 위협조로, 험악하게)
Dark looks or remarks make you think that the person giving them wants to harm you or that something horrible is going to happen.

Chapter 5

1. **How did Arthur feel about playing as a dinosaur?**

   A. He wished that he could join Binky and Francine.

   B. He wished that he could be a real dinosaur instead.

   C. He was not in the mood to play dinosaur.

   D. He thought it would cheer up Buster.

2. **Why was Arthur nervous?**

   A. He thought that they might break the fossil.

   B. He thought that they would get caught with the fossil.

   C. He thought that they would get home late from the field trip.

   D. He thought that they would get a bad grade for the field trip.

3. How had Buster reacted to Muffy bringing goat cheese to class in the past?

A. He had insisted it was fake because he had never heard of it.

B. He had insisted it was bad because it smelled funny.

C. He had insisted that she share it, because he had never eaten it.

D. He had insisted it was a way for her to show off her wealth.

4. Why did Arthur think Ranger Ruth was coming for him?

A. He thought that she would frisk them for the fossil.

B. He thought that she would let them keep the fossil.

C. He thought that she would hire Buster as a paleontologist.

D. He thought that she would tell them to give up looking for fossils.

5. What did Ranger Ruth tell Buster before he left?

A. She told him that she knew he had stolen a fossil.

B. She told him to return the fossil when he felt like it.

C. She told him to not be discouraged about his fossil hunting.

D. She told him that she was glad that they enjoyed their time.

1분에 몇 단어를 읽는지 리딩 속도를 측정해보세요.

$$\frac{522 \text{ words}}{\text{reading time (\quad) sec}} \times 60 = (\qquad) \text{ WPM}$$

Build Your Vocabulary

growl [graul] v. 으르렁거리다; 으르렁거리듯 말하다; n. 으르렁거리는 소리
When a dog or other animal growls, it makes a low noise in its throat, usually because it is angry.

claw [klɔː] v. (손톱·발톱으로) 할퀴다; n. (동물의) 발톱; 갈고리 모양의 도구
If an animal claws at something, it scratches or damages it with its claws.

swoop [swuːp] v. 급강하하다; 급습하다; n. 급강하; 급습
When a bird or airplane swoops, it suddenly moves downward through the air in a smooth curving movement.

mood [muːd] n. 기분; 분위기
Your mood is the way you are feeling at a particular time.

nervous [nə́ːrvəs] a. 불안해하는, 초조해하는; 겁을 잘 먹는
If someone is nervous, they are frightened or worried about something that is happening or might happen, and show this in their behavior.

get away with idiom (벌 등을) 교묘히 모면하다; ~을 잘 해내다
If you are saying that someone gets away with something, you mean they do something wrong and are not punished or criticized for it.

credit [krédit] n. 칭찬, 인정; 신용 거래; v. ~을 ~로 여기다; ~를 ~의 공으로 믿다
If you get the credit for something good, people praise you because you are responsible for it, or are thought to be responsible for it.

belong [bilɔ́:ŋ] v. 제자리에 있다; ~에 속하다; 소속감을 느끼다
If a person or thing belongs in a particular place or situation, that is where they should be.

give up idiom 단념하다, 그만두다, 포기하다
If you give something up, you stop trying to do it or having it.

squeeze [skwi:z] v. (꼭) 짜다, 쥐다; (좁은 곳에) 밀어 넣다; n. 짜기
If you squeeze something, you press it firmly, usually with your hands.

piece [pi:s] n. 한 부분, 조각; 한 개
A piece of something can refer to a single instance of a particular type.

history [hístəri] n. 역사; 역사(학)
You can refer to the events of the past as history. You can also refer to the past events which concern a particular topic or place as its history.

arrest [ərést] v. 체포하다; 막다, 저지하다; n. 체포; 저지, 정지 (arrested a. 체포된)
If the police arrest you, they take charge of you and take you to a police station, because they believe you may have committed a crime.

detector [ditéktər] n. 탐지기
A detector is an instrument which is used to discover that something is present somewhere, or to measure how much of something there is.

alarm [əlá:rm] n. 경보장치; 불안, 공포; v. 불안하게 하다; 경보장치를 달다
An alarm is an automatic device that warns you of danger, for example by ringing a bell.

insist [insíst] v. 고집하다, 주장하다, 우기다
If you insist that something is the case, you say so very firmly and refuse to say otherwise, even though other people do not believe you.

fake [feik] a. 가짜의, 거짓의; 모조의; n. 모조품; v. 위조하다; ~인 척하다
A fake fur or a fake painting, for example, is a fur or painting that has been made to look valuable or genuine, usually in order to deceive people.

make sense idiom 타당하다; 의미가 통하다, 이해가 되다
If a course of action makes sense, it seems sensible.

tin [tin] n. (= tin can) (통조림) 통; 깡통; 주석
A tin is a metal container which is filled with food and sealed in order to preserve the food for long periods of time.

invent [invént] v. 발명하다; (사실이 아닌 것을) 지어내다
If you invent something such as a machine or process, you are the first person to think of it or make it.

realistic [riːəlístik] a. 사실적인; 현실성 있는; 현실적인
You say that a painting, story, or film is realistic when the people and things in it are like people and things in real life.

base [beis] v. 바탕을 두다; 기초로 하다; n. 기초, 근거; 토대 (**based** a. ~에 기반을 둔)
If you base one thing on another thing, the first thing develops from the second thing.

tweet [twiːt] n. 짹짹 (하고 작은 새가 우는 소리); 높은 음
A tweet is a short, high-pitched sound made by a small bird.

blow [blou] v. (악기 등을) 불다; 입김을 내뿜다; (바람·입김에) 날리다; n. 바람; 강타
When a whistle or horn blows or someone blows it, they make a sound by blowing into it.

whistle [hwisl] n. 호루라기 (소리); 휘파람; v. 휘파람을 불다; 호루라기를 불다
A whistle is a small metal tube which you blow in order to produce a loud sound and attract someone's attention.

gather [gǽðər] v. (사람들이) 모이다; (여기 저기 있는 것을) 모으다
If people gather somewhere or if someone gathers people somewhere, they come together in a group.

belonging [bilɔ́ːŋiŋ] n. (pl.) 소지품, 소유물, 재산
Your belongings are the things that you own, especially things that are small enough to be carried.

rough [rʌf] a. 매끈하지 않은, 거친; 개략적인; (행동이) 난폭한
If a surface is rough, it is uneven and not smooth.

outline [áutlàin] n. 윤곽; 개요; v. 개요를 서술하다; 윤곽을 보여주다
The outline of something is its general shape, especially when it cannot
be clearly seen.

footprint [fútprìnt] n. (사람·동물의) 발자국
A footprint is a mark in the shape of a foot that a person or animal makes
in or on a surface.

ranger [réindʒər] n. 삼림 관리원
A ranger is a person whose job is to look after a forest or large park.

frisk [frisk] v. 몸수색을 하다; 뛰놀다, 뛰어 다니다
If someone frisks you, they search you, usually with their hands in order
to see if you are hiding a weapon or something else such as drugs in
your clothes.

trigger [trígər] v. (장치를) 작동시키다; 촉발시키다; n. (총의) 방아쇠
To trigger a bomb or system means to cause it to work.

hiss [his] v. 쉿 하고 말하다, (화난 어조로) 낮게 말하다; n. 쉬 하는 소리; 쉭쉭거리는 야유
If you hiss something, you say it forcefully in a whisper.

detect [ditékt] v. 발견하다, 알아내다, 감지하다 (detection n. 발견, 탐지)
Detection is the discovery of something which is supposed to be hidden.

net [net] n. 그물, 망; 망사; v. 그물로 잡다; 그물을 치다
A net is a piece of netting which is used for catching fish, insects, or
animals.

goner [gɔ́:nər] n. (살리거나 구할) 가망이 없는 사람
If you say that someone is a goner, you mean that they are about to die,
or are in such danger that nobody can save them.

brighten [braitn] v. (얼굴 등이) 환해지다; 밝아지다
If someone brightens or their face brightens, they suddenly look happier.

at once idiom 즉시, 당장; 동시에, 한꺼번에
If you do something at once, you do it immediately.

comfortable [kʌ́mfərtəbl] a. 편안한, 쾌적한; 편하게 생각하는; 넉넉한
(uncomfortable a. 불편한, 거북한)
If you are uncomfortable, you are slightly worried or embarrassed, and not relaxed and confident.

pat [pæt] v. 쓰다듬다, 토닥거리다; n. 쓰다듬기
If you pat something or someone, you tap them lightly, usually with your hand held flat.

discourage [diskɔ́ːridʒ] v. 의욕을 꺾다, 좌절시키다; 막다, 말리다
(discouraged a. 낙담한, 낙심한)
If someone or something discourages you, they cause you to lose your enthusiasm about your actions.

have the makings of idiom ~이 될 자질을 갖추고 있다
If you say that someone has the makings of something, you mean that they have the necessary qualities or character to become it.

paleontologist [peiliəntá:lədʒist] n. 고생물학자
A paleontologist is a specialist in paleontology which is the earth science that studies fossil organisms and related remains.

Chapter

6

1. **With whom did Buster say that Arthur could talk about the fossil?**
   A. Nobody
   B. Buster's mother
   C. Only Buster's friends
   D. Francine and the Brain

2. **What did Buster do with the fossil when he got home?**
   A. He showed it off to his mother.
   B. He hid it under the dining room table.
   C. He put it in a shoe box and put the box in his closet.
   D. He put it under the pillow on the bed in his room.

3. What did Buster's mom say about his mashed potatoes?

A. She said that he should add butter to them.

B. She said it looked like a dinosaur footprint.

C. She said that Buster could have more later.

D. She said that Buster should stop playing with his food.

4. Which of the following did NOT come to Buster's home in his dream?

A. A tyrannosaurus with Binky's head

B. A triceratops with Francine's head

C. A large dinosaur

D. Ranger Ruth

5. Why had they come to Buster's home in his dream?

A. They wanted to just see Binky.

B. They wanted to take the footprint back.

C. They wanted Buster to show them how to find fossils.

D. They wanted Buster to come on an adventure with them.

1분에 몇 단어를 읽는지 리딩 속도를 측정해보세요.

$$\frac{512 \ words}{reading \ time \ (\quad) \ sec} \times 60 = (\quad) \ WPM$$

Build Your Vocabulary

fossil [fásəl] n. 화석
A fossil is the hard remains of a prehistoric animal or plant that are found inside a rock.

shade [ʃeid] n. (= window shade) (창문에 치는) 블라인드; 그늘; v. 그늘지게 하다
A window shade is a piece of stiff cloth or heavy paper that you can pull down over a window as a covering.

perimeter [pərímitər] n. (어떤 구역의) 주위, 주변
The perimeter of an area of land is the whole of its outer edge or boundary.

security [sikjúərəti] n. 보안, 경비; 안도감, 안심
Security refers to all the measures that are taken to protect a place, or to ensure that only people with permission enter it or leave it.

in place idiom ~을 위한 준비가 되어 있는; 제자리에 있는
If something is in place, it is prepared and ready.

wrap [ræp] v. (보호 등을 하기 위해) 싸다; 포장하다; (무엇의 둘레를) 두르다; n. 포장지
When you wrap something, you fold paper or cloth tightly round it to cover it completely, for example in order to protect it or so that you can give it to someone as a present.

tinfoil [tínfɔil] n. (식품포장 등에 쓰이는) 은박지
Tinfoil consists of shiny metal in the form of a thin sheet which is used for wrapping food.

phase [feiz] n. (변화·발달 과정상의 한) 단계; v. 단계적으로 하다
A phase is a particular stage in a process or in the gradual development of something.

fill [fil] v. (가득) 채우다; (구멍·틈을) 때우다; n. 실컷; (음식·술을) 양껏
If you fill a container or area, or if it fills, an amount of something enters it that is enough to make it full.

rest [rest] n. 나머지 (사람들·것들); 휴식; v. 쉬다; 기대다
The rest is used to refer to all the parts of something or all the things in a group that remain or that you have not already mentioned.

marble [ma:rbl] n. (아이들이 가지고 노는) 구슬; 대리석
A marble is one of the small balls used in the game.

bowl [boul] n. 그릇, 사발; 한 그릇의 분량
A bowl is a round container with a wide uncovered top.

shelf [ʃelf] n. 선반; 책꽂이, (책장의) 칸
A shelf is a flat piece which is attached to a wall or to the sides of a cupboard for keeping things on.

closet [klázit] n. 벽장
A closet is a piece of furniture with doors at the front and shelves inside, which is used for storing things.

set [set] v. (set–set) (시계·기기를) 맞추다; (해·달이) 지다; a. 위치한; 정해진
When you set a clock or control, you adjust it to a particular point or level.

alert [əló:rt] n. 경계 태세; a. 경계하는; v. (위험 등을) 알리다; 의식하게 하다
An alert is a situation in which people prepare themselves for something dangerous that might happen soon.

status [stéitəs] n. 상황; 신분, 자격; 지위
The status of something is its state of affairs at a particular time.

confirm [kənfó:rm] v. 더 분명히 해 주다; 확인해 주다
If you confirm an arrangement or appointment, you say that it is definite, usually in a letter or on the telephone.

awful [ɔ́:fəl] a. 엄청; 끔찍한, 지독한 (**awfully** ad. 정말, 몹시)
You can use awful with adjectives that describe a quality in order to emphasize that particular quality.

trip [trip] n. 여행; 발을 헛디딤; v. 발을 헛디디다; ~를 넘어뜨리다 (**field trip** n. 현장 학습)
A trip is a journey that you make to a particular place.

knock [nak] v. 치다, 부딪치다; (문을) 두드리다; n. 문 두드리는 소리; 부딪침
If you knock something, you touch or hit it roughly, especially so that it falls or moves.

friendly [fréndli] a. 친절한, 우호적인
If someone is friendly, they behave in a pleasant, kind way, and like to be with other people.

nod [nad] v. (고개를) 끄덕이다, 끄덕여 나타내다; n. (고개를) 끄덕임
If you nod, you move your head downward and upward to show agreement, understanding, or approval.

pause [pɔːz] v. (말·일을 하다가) 잠시 멈추다; 정지시키다; n. 멈춤
If you pause while you are doing something, you stop for a short period and then continue.

dinosaur [dáinəsɔːr] n. 공룡
Dinosaurs were large reptiles which lived in prehistoric times.

roll one's eyes idiom 눈을 굴리다
If you roll your eyes, they move round and upward when they are frightened, bored, or annoyed.

mash [mæʃ] v. (음식을 부드럽게) 으깨다; n. 으깨 놓은 것
If you mash food that is solid but soft, you crush it so that it forms a soft mass.

plate [pleit] n. 접시, 그릇; (자동차) 번호판; 판, 패 v. 판을 대다
A plate is a round or oval flat dish that is used to hold food.

go on idiom 말을 계속하다; (어떤 상황이) 계속되다; 시작하다
When you go on, you continue speaking after a short pause.

scoop [sku:p] v. 뜨다, 파다; 재빨리 들어올리다; n. 국자; 한 숟갈
If you scoop something from a container, you remove it with something such as a spoon.

bite [bait] n. 한 입; 물기; v. (이빨로) 물다
If you have a bite to eat, you have a small meal or a snack.

swallow [swálou] v. (음식 등을) 삼키다; 마른침을 삼키다; n. 삼키기; [동물] 제비
If you swallow something, you cause it to go from your mouth down into your stomach.

design [dizáin] n. 무늬; 디자인; 설계; v. 도안하다; 설계하다
A design is a pattern of lines, flowers, or shapes which is used to decorate something.

toss and turn idiom 뒤척이다
If you toss and turn, you keep moving around in bed and cannot sleep properly, for example because you are ill or worried.

thump [θʌmp] n. 쿵 (하는 소리); v. (세게) 치다; 쿵 하고 떨어지다
A thump is a loud, dull sound by hitting something.

wonder [wʌ́ndər] v. 궁금해하다; (크게) 놀라다; n. 경탄, 경이
If you wonder about something, you think about it because it interests you and you want to know more about it.

confuse [kənfjú:z] v. 혼동하다; (사람을) 혼란시키다
If you confuse two things, you get them mixed up, so that you think one of them is the other one.

ignore [ignɔ́:r] v. 무시하다, 못 본척하다
If you ignore someone or something, you pay no attention to them.

fool [fu:l] v. 속이다, 기만하다; 바보 짓을 하다; n. 바보
If someone fools you, they deceive or trick you.

flick [flik] v. 휙 움직이다; (손가락 등으로) 튀기다; n. 휙 움직임
If something flicks in a particular direction, or if someone flicks it, it moves with a short, sudden movement.

slam [slæm] v. 쾅 닫다; 세게 놓다; n. 탕 하고 닫기; 탕 하는 소리
If you slam a door or window or if it slams, it shuts noisily and with great force.

tumble [tʌmbl] v. 굴러 떨어지다; 폭삭 무너지다; n. 굴러 떨어짐; 폭락
If someone or something tumbles somewhere, they fall there with a rolling or bouncing movement.

spill [spil] v. 쏟아지다, 흘리다; 쏟아져 나오다; n. 유출; 흘린 액체
If the contents of a bag, box, or other container spill or are spilled, they come out of the container onto a surface.

grab [græb] v. 붙잡다, 움켜잡다; n. 와락 잡아채려고 함
If you grab something, you take it or pick it up suddenly and roughly.

tremble [trembl] v. (가볍게) 흔들리다; (몸을) 떨다; n. 떨림, 전율
If something trembles, it shakes slightly.

Chapter

7

1. **What was the worst part of Buster's dream?**

   A. That he had to still go to school

   B. That the fossil got him into trouble

   C. That Francine had sharp dinosaur teeth

   D. That Binky's head looked natural on the tyrannosaurus

2. **What did Buster think his dream was telling him?**

   A. That he should return the fossil

   B. That he should tell his other friends about the fossil

   C. That he should not put so much chocolate on pie

   D. That he should not try to be a paleontologist

3. When did Buster tell Arthur that he could come over and see the fossil?

    A. Never

    B. After school

    C. On the weekends

    D. Only when Buster was home

4. Why did Francine think that Buster had not slept well?

    A. She thought that he had watched too much TV.

    B. She thought that he felt bad about keeping the fossil a secret.

    C. She thought that he felt sick from eating too much ice cream.

    D. She thought that he felt bad about not finding anything.

5. What kind of fossils were rare according to Mr. Ratburn?

    A. Dinosaur toes

    B. Dinosaur teeth

    C. Dinosaur bones

    D. Dinosaur footprints

$$\frac{497 \text{ words}}{\text{reading time ( ) sec}} \times 60 = (\quad) \text{ WPM}$$

Build Your Vocabulary

: **relate** [riléit] v. ~에 대하여 이야기하다; 관련시키다, 결부시키다
If you relate a story, you tell it.

: **detail** [ditéil] n. 세부 사항; v. 상세히 알리다, 열거하다
The details of something are its individual features or elements.

. **nightmare** [náitmɛər] n. 악몽; 아주 끔찍한 일
A nightmare is a very frightening dream.

: **consider** [kənsídər] v. 고려하다, 숙고하다; 여기다
If you consider something, you think about it carefully.

. **sauce** [sɔːs] n. (요리용) 소스
A sauce is a thick liquid which is served with other food.

. **stomachache** [stʌ́məkeik] n. 위통, 복통
If you have a stomachache, you have a pain in your stomach.

bedtime [bédtàim] n. 취침 시간, 잠자리에 드는 시간
Your bedtime is the time when you usually go to bed.

. **sigh** [sai] v. 한숨을 쉬다, 한숨짓다; n. 한숨; 탄식
When you sigh, you let out a deep breath, as a way of expressing feelings such as disappointment, tiredness, or pleasure.

come over idiom (특히 누구의 집에) 들르다; (어떤 기분이) 갑자기 들다
When you come over to some place, you visit someone for a short time, usually at their home.

security [sikjúərəti] n. 보안, 경비; 안도감, 안심
Security refers to all the measures that are taken to protect a place, or to ensure that only people with permission enter it or leave it.

arrange [əréindʒ] v. 마련하다, (일을) 처리하다; 정리하다, 배열하다
(arrangement n. (처리) 방식; 준비)
Arrangements are plans and preparations which you make so that something will happen or be possible.

disturb [distə́:rb] v. (제자리에 있는 것을) 건드리다; 방해하다
If something is disturbed, its position or shape is changed.

insist [insíst] v. 고집하다, 주장하다, 우기다
If you insist that something should be done, you say so very firmly and refuse to give in about it.

point [pɔint] n. 의미; 요점; v. (손가락 등으로) 가리키다; (길을) 알려 주다
If you ask what the point of something is, or say that there is no point in it, you are indicating that a particular action has no purpose or would not be useful.

expert [ékspə:rt] n. 전문가; a. 전문가의, 전문적인; 숙련된
An expert is a person who is very skilled at doing something or who knows a lot about a particular subject.

paleontologist [peiliəntálədʒist] n. 고생물학자
A paleontologist is a specialist in paleontology which is the earth science that studies fossil organisms and related remains.

knowledge [nálidʒ] n. 지식; (특정 사실·상황에 대해) 알고 있음
Knowledge is information and understanding about a subject, which a person has, or which all people have.

tool [tu:l] n. 도구, 연장; 수단
A tool is any instrument or simple piece of equipment that you hold in your hands and use to do a particular kind of work.

fair [fɛər] a. 공정한; 타당한; 아름다운; n. 박람회
Something or someone that is fair is reasonable, right, and just.

stare [stɛər] v. 빤히 쳐다보다, 응시하다; n. 빤히 쳐다보기, 응시
If you stare at someone or something, you look at them for a long time.

trip [trip] n. 여행; 발을 헛디딤; v. 발을 헛디디다; ~를 넘어뜨리다 (field trip n. 현장 학습)
A trip is a journey that you make to a particular place.

amazing [əméiziŋ] a. (감탄스럽도록) 놀라운, 멋진
You say that something is amazing when it is very surprising and makes you feel pleasure, approval, or wonder.

sign [sain] n. 흔적, 징후; 몸짓; v. 서명하다; 신호를 보내다
If there is a sign of something, there is something which shows that it exists or is happening.

fidget [fídʒit] v. 꼼지락거리다, 가만히 못 있다; n. 안절부절못함
If you fidget, you keep moving your hands or feet slightly or changing your position slightly, for example because you are nervous, bored, or excited.

cover [kávər] v. 씌우다, 가리다; 덮다; n. (책이나 잡지의) 표지; 덮개
If you cover something, you place something else over it in order to protect it, hide it, or close it.

rare [rɛər] a. (rarer−rarest) 드문, 보기 힘든; 진귀한, 희귀한
Something that is rare is not common and is therefore interesting or valuable.

footprint [fútprìnt] n. (사람·동물의) 발자국
A footprint is a mark in the shape of a foot that a person or animal makes in or on a surface.

shrug [ʃrʌg] v. (어깨를) 으쓱하다; n. (어깨를) 으쓱하기
If you shrug, you raise your shoulders to show that you are not interested in something or that you do not know or care about something.

groan [groun] v. 신음 소리를 내다, 끙끙거리다; n. 신음, 끙 하는 소리
If you groan, you make a long, low sound because you are in pain, or because you are upset or unhappy about something.

throughout [θruːáut] prep. ~동안 죽, 내내; 도처에
If you say that something happens throughout a particular period of time, you mean that it happens during the whole of that period.

history [hístəri] n. 역사; 역사(학)
You can refer to the events of the past as history. You can also refer to the past events which concern a particular topic or place as its history.

disappoint [disəpɔ́int] v. 실망시키다; 좌절시키다 (disappointment n. 실망, 낙심)
If things or people disappoint you, they are not as good as you had hoped, or do not do what you hoped they would do.

triumph [tráiəmf] v. 승리를 거두다, 이기다; n. 승리, 대성공
If someone or something triumphs, they gain complete success, control, or victory, often after a long or difficult struggle.

slump [slʌmp] v. 털썩 앉다; 급감하다, 급락하다; n. 급감, 폭락; 불황
If you slump somewhere, you fall or sit down there heavily, for example because you are very tired or you feel ill.

Chapter

8

1. What did Mrs. Baxter think was the cause of Buster looking tired?

A. She thought he might be sad about his field trip.

B. She thought he might be having problems at school.

C. She thought he might be having problems with her.

D. She thought he might be overeating.

2. Why did Buster think that Arthur was calling about the fossil when he asked a math question?

A. Because he asked about coming over for help.

B. Because he asked about hidden things.

C. Because he asked about measuring fossils.

D. Because he asked about measuring by the "foot."

3. What did Buster tell his mother was in the shoebox?

    A. His secret toy collection

    B. His comic collection

    C. His school project

    D. His secret fossil

4. Which of the following did NOT show up in Buster's dream?

    A. A police officer

    B. A triceratops

    C. Ranger Ruth

    D. Arthur

5. What did they think Buster was hiding in his room?

    A. A living dinosaur

    B. A fossil from the park

    C. Arthur's homework

    D. An overdue library book

1분에 몇 단어를 읽는지 리딩 속도를 측정해보세요.

$$\frac{482 \text{ words}}{\text{reading time ( ) sec}} \times 60 = (\quad) \text{ WPM}$$

Build Your Vocabulary

be supposed to idiom ~하기로 되어있다; ~해야 한다
If you are supposed to do something, you are required to do it because of the position you are in or an agreement you have made.

measure [méʒər] v. 측정하다, 재다; 판단하다; n. 조치; 척도, 기준
If you measure a quantity that can be expressed in numbers, such as the length of something, you discover it using a particular instrument or device, for example a ruler.

fool [fuːl] v. 속이다, 기만하다; 바보 짓을 하다; n. 바보
If someone fools you, they deceive or trick you.

check up on idiom ~을 확인하다
If you check up on something, you find out if something is true or correct.

honestly [ánistli] ad. 정말로, 진짜로; 솔직히
You use honestly to emphasize that you are telling the truth and that you want people to believe you.

hang up idiom 전화를 끊다, 수화기를 놓다
If you hang up the phone, you end a telephone conversation, often very suddenly.

rush [rʌʃ] v. 급히 움직이다, 서두르다; 재촉하다; n. 혼잡, 분주함; (감정이) 치밀어 오름
If you rush somewhere, you go there quickly.

project [prádʒekt] n. 과제; 계획, 기획; v. 계획하다; (빛·영상 등을) 비추다
A project is a detailed study of a subject by a pupil or student.

delicate [délikət] a. 연약한, 부서지기 쉬운; 정교한; 미묘한, 까다로운
If something is delicate, it is easy to harm, damage, or break, and needs
to be handled or treated carefully.

hush-hush [hʌ́ʃ-hʌ̀ʃ] a. 극비의; 쉬쉬하는
Something that is hush-hush is secret and not to be discussed with other
people.

top secret [tap síːkrit] a. 일급비밀의, 극비의
Top secret information or activity is intended to be kept completely
secret, for example in order to prevent a country's enemies from finding
out about it.

closet [klázit] n. 벽장
A closet is a piece of furniture with doors at the front and shelves inside,
which is used for storing things.

concern [kənsə́ːrn] v. ~를 걱정스럽게 하다; 영향을 미치다 n. 우려; 배려
(concerned a. 걱정하는, 염려하는)
If something concerns you, it worries you.

rest [rest] n. 휴식; 나머지 (사람들·것들); v. 쉬다; 기대다
If you get some rest or have a rest, you do not do anything active for
a time.

glance [glæns] v. 흘낏 보다; 대충 훑어보다; n. 흘낏 봄
If you glance at something or someone, you look at them very quickly
and then look away again immediately.

squeak [skwiːk] v. 꽥 소리치다; 끽 하는 소리를 내다; n. 끼익 하는 소리
If something or someone squeaks, they make a short, high-pitched
sound.

fossil [fásəl] n. 화석
A fossil is the hard remains of a prehistoric animal or plant that are found
inside a rock.

eyelid [áilid] n. 눈꺼풀
Your eyelids are the two pieces of skin which cover your eyes when they are closed.

droop [druːp] v. 아래로 처지다, 늘어지다; 풀이 죽다
If something droops, it hangs or leans downward with no strength or firmness.

knock [nak] n. 문 두드리는 소리; 부딪침; v. 치다, 부딪치다; (문을) 두드리다
A knock is a sudden short noise made when someone or something hits a door.

burst [bəːrst] v. (burst-burst) 불쑥 움직이다; 터지다, 파열하다; n. (갑자기) 한바탕 ~을 함
When a door or lid bursts open, it opens very suddenly and violently because someone pushes it or there is great pressure behind it.

ranger [réindʒər] n. 삼림 관리원
A ranger is a person whose job is to look after a forest or large park.

drag [dræg] v. 끌다, 끌고 가다; 힘들게 움직이다; n. 끌기; 장애물
If someone drags you somewhere, they pull you there, or force you to go there by physically threatening you.

stripe [straip] n. 줄무늬 (striped a. 줄무늬가 있는)
A stripe is a long line which is a different color from the areas next to it.

prisoner [prízənər] n. 재소자, 죄수; 포로
A prisoner is a person who is kept in a prison as a punishment for a crime that they have committed.

uniform [júːnəfɔ̀ːrm] n. 제복, 군복, 교복, 유니폼; a. 획일적인, 균일한
A uniform is a special set of clothes which some people, for example soldiers or the police, wear to work in and which some children wear at school.

tickle [tikl] v. 간지럼을 태우다; 간질이다; n. 간지럽히기; 간지러움
When you tickle someone, you move your fingers lightly over a sensitive part of their body, often in order to make them laugh.

defend [difénd] v. 방어하다, 수비하다; 옹호하다, 변호하다
If you defend someone or something, you take action in order to protect them.

handcuff [hǽndkʌf] n. 수갑; v. 수갑을 채우다
Handcuffs are two metal rings which are joined together and can be locked round someone's wrists, usually by the police during an arrest.

treat [tri:t] v. 대하다, 다루다; 치료하다, 처치하다; n. 대접
(treatment n. 대우, 처리; 치료)
Your treatment of someone is the way you behave toward them or deal with them.

dinosaur [dáinəsɔːr] n. 공룡
Dinosaurs were large reptiles which lived in prehistoric times.

dart [da:rt] v. 휙 눈길을 던지다; 쏜살같이 움직이다; n. (작은) 화살; 쏜살같이 움직임
If you dart a look at someone or something, or if your eyes dart to them, you look at them very quickly.

ridiculous [ridíkjuləs] a. 말도 안 되는, 터무니없는, 웃기는
If you say that something or someone is ridiculous, you mean that they are very foolish.

gaze [geiz] n. 응시, 시선; v. 가만히 응시하다, 바라보다
You can talk about someone's gaze as a way of describing how they are looking at something, especially when they are looking steadily at it.

halt [hɔ:lt] v. 멈추다, 서다; 중단시키다; n. 멈춤, 중단
When a person or a vehicle halts or when something halts them, they stop moving in the direction they were going and stand still.

strange [streindʒ] a. 이상한; 낯선
Something that is strange is unusual or unexpected, and makes you feel slightly nervous or afraid.

tromp [trɔmp] n. (저벅저벅 걷는) 발자국 소리; v. 터벅터벅 걷다
The tromp of people is the sound of their heavy, regular walking.

be about to idiom 막 ~하려던 참이다
If you are about to do something, you are going to do it immediately.

roar [rɔːr] v. 으르렁거리다; 고함치다; n. 으르렁거림; 함성; 굉음
If something roars, it makes a very loud noise.

: **guilty** [gílti] a. 유죄의; 죄책감이 드는, 가책을 느끼는
If someone is guilty of a crime or offence, they have committed that crime or offence.

: **charge** [ʧɑːrdʒ] v. 기소하다; 비난하다; 달려가다; 청구하다; n. 요금; 책임, 담당
When the police charge someone, they formally accuse them of having done something illegal.

be cooped up idiom (좁은 곳에) 가두다
If a person or an animal is cooped up, they/it are kept in a small place or inside a building.

Chapter 9

1. **Why did Arthur go to Buster's place on his way home?**

   A. Arthur had to drop off Buster's school work.

   B. Arthur wanted to study together with Buster.

   C. Buster had called Arthur earlier with a problem.

   D. Buster had missed school and Arthur wanted to go by.

2. **How was Buster's room when Arthur arrived?**

   A. It was spotlessly clean.

   B. It was completely empty.

   C. It was a mess.

   D. It was locked.

3. What did Buster think was part of the dinosaurs' master plan?

A. That the dinosaurs wanted people to think they were extinct.

B. That the dinosaurs wanted people to be afraid of them.

C. That the dinosaurs would make a better world.

D. That the fossils would come back to life.

4. How did Buster first think having the fossil would make him feel?

A. Smart and clever

B. Special and important

C. Brave and strong

D. Practical and useful

5. What did Arthur say about the fossil in the end?

A. It belonged at Arthur's house.

B. It belonged at school.

C. It didn't belong in a museum.

D. It didn't belong at Busters or Arthur's house.

1분에 몇 단어를 읽는지 리딩 속도를 측정해보세요.

$$\frac{467 \ words}{reading \ time \ (\quad) \ sec} \times 60 = (\quad) \ WPM$$

Build Your Vocabulary

absent [ǽbsənt] a. 결석한, 결근한; 멍한; v. 결석하다, 불참하다
If someone or something is absent from a place or situation where they should be or where they usually are, they are not there.

figure [fígjər] v. 생각하다, 판단하다; 중요하다; n. 수치; (멀리서 흐릿하게 보이는) 모습
If you figure that something is the case, you think or guess that it is the case.

sigh [sai] v. 한숨을 쉬다, 한숨짓다; n. 한숨; 탄식
When you sigh, you let out a deep breath, as a way of expressing feelings such as disappointment, tiredness, or pleasure.

contagious [kəntéidʒəs] a. 전염되는, 전염성의; 전염병에 걸린
A disease that is contagious can be caught by touching people or things that are infected with it.

reach [ri:ʧ] v. 이르다, 도달하다; (손·팔을) 뻗다, 내밀다; n. 거리; 범위
When someone or something reaches a place, they arrive there.

knock [nak] v. (문을) 두드리다; 치다, 부딪치다; n. 문 두드리는 소리; 부딪침
If you knock on something such as a door or window, you hit it, usually several times, to attract someone's attention.

pajamas [pədʒáːməz] n. (바지와 상의로 된) 잠옷
A pair of pajamas consists of loose trousers and a loose jacket that people wear in bed.

just in time idiom 마침 좋은 때에; 겨우 시간에 맞춰
If you are just in time for a particular event, you make your appearance
for it in good timing or are not too late for it.

prepare [pripéər] v. 준비하다; 대비하다, 각오하다 (preparation n. 준비, 대비)
Preparations are all the arrangements that are made for a future event.

blink [bliŋk] v. 눈을 깜박이다; (불빛이) 깜박거리다; n. 눈을 깜박거림
When you blink or when you blink your eyes, you shut your eyes and
very quickly open them again.

mess [mes] n. (지저분하고) 엉망인 상태; 엉망인 상황; v. 엉망으로 만들다
If you say that something is a mess or in a mess, you think that it is in
an untidy state.

closet [klázit] n. 벽장
A closet is a piece of furniture with doors at the front and shelves inside,
which is used for storing things.

web [web] n. 거미줄; (복잡하게 연결된) 망
A web is the thin net made by a spider from a sticky substance which
it produces in its body.

string [striŋ] n. 끈, 줄; 일련; v. (끈이나 줄로) 묶다; (실 등에) 꿰다
String is thin rope made of twisted threads, used for tying things together
or tying up parcels.

crisscross [krískrɔ̀ːs] v. 교차하다; 십자를 그리다; n. 열십자, 십자형
If two sets of lines or things crisscross, they cross over each other.

point [pɔint] v. (손가락 등으로) 가리키다; (길을) 알려 주다; n. 의미; 요점
If you point at a person or thing, you hold out your finger toward them
in order to make someone notice them.

detector [ditéktər] n. 탐지기
A detector is an instrument which is used to discover that something
is present somewhere, or to measure how much of something there is.

extinct [ikstíŋkt] a. 멸종된; 더 이상 존재하지 않는, 사라진
A species of animal or plant that is extinct no longer has any living members, either in the world or in a particular place.

master plan [mǽstər plæn] n. 기본 설계, 종합 계획
A master plan is a clever plan that is intended to help someone succeed in a very difficult or important task.

nod [nad] v. (고개를) 끄덕이다, 끄덕여 나타내다; n. (고개를) 끄덕임
If you nod, you move your head downward and upward to show agreement, understanding, or approval.

trick [trik] v. 속이다, 속임수를 쓰다; n. 속임수; 장난; 묘기; a. 교묘한
If someone tricks you, they deceive you, often in order to make you do something.

fool [fuːl] v. 속이다, 기만하다; 바보 짓을 하다; n. 바보
If someone fools you, they deceive or trick you.

go overboard idiom 잔뜩 흥분하다, 야단을 피우다
If you say that someone goes overboard, you mean that they do something to a greater extent than is necessary or reasonable.

snort [snɔːrt] v. 코웃음을 치다, 콧방귀를 뀌다; n. 코웃음, 콧방귀
If someone snorts something, they say it in a way that shows contempt.

scary [skέəri] a. 무서운, 겁나는
Something that is scary is rather frightening.

rub [rʌb] v. 문지르다; (두 손 등을) 맞비비다; n. 문지르기, 비비기
If you rub a part of your body, you move your hand or fingers backward and forward over it while pressing firmly.

get rid of idiom ~을 처리하다, 없애다
When you get rid of something that you do not want or do not like, you take action so that you no longer have it or suffer from it.

guilty [gílti] a. 죄책감이 드는, 가책을 느끼는; 유죄의
If you feel guilty, you feel unhappy because you think that you have done something wrong or have failed to do something which you should have done.

pace [peis] v. 서성거리다; (일의) 속도를 유지하다; n. 속도; 걸음
If you pace a small area, you keep walking up and down it, because you are anxious or impatient.

back and forth idiom 앞뒤로; 좌우로; 여기저기에, 왔다 갔다
If someone moves back and forth, they repeatedly move in one direction and then in the opposite direction.

nuts [nʌts] a. 미친, 제정신이 아닌 (drive someone nuts idiom ~를 미치게 하다)
If someone or something drives you nuts, they make you very annoyed.

stare [stɛər] v. 빤히 쳐다보다, 응시하다; n. 빤히 쳐다보기, 응시
If you stare at someone or something, you look at them for a long time.

belong [bilɔ́:ŋ] v. 제자리에 있다; ~에 속하다; 소속감을 느끼다
If a person or thing belongs in a particular place or situation, that is where they should be.

give a look idiom 표정을 짓다; ~를 보다
If you give someone a look, you twist your face to express your feeling or emotion or simply look at them.

Chapter

10

1. **What were Arthur and Buster waiting for at the Rainbow Rock Visitor Center?**

   A. They were waiting to take the fossil back.

   B. They were waiting for information about the fossil.

   C. They were waiting for a chance to steal another fossil.

   D. They were waiting for their punishment for stealing a fossil.

2. **How did Ranger Ruth feel about Buster and Arthur returning the fossil?**

   A. She wished that they had kept the fossil for themselves.

   B. She called the police to have them arrested for stealing.

   C. She was pleased and went easy on them.

   D. She wanted to punish them harshly.

3. Why did Ranger Ruth go easy on Buster?

A. She heard about the nightmares.

B. She talked with Buster's mom.

C. She knew from the start that he had taken the fossil.

D. She wanted Buster to work at the museum in the future.

4. Which of Buster's tools did he say especially helped him?

A. The fossil detector

B. The chisels

C. The shovel

D. The pith helmet

5. What did Ranger Ruth want to show Buster and Arthur?

A. A new dinosaur statue

B. A recently discovered fossil

C. A brass plaque with their names

D. A photo of the dinosaur that made the footprint

1분에 몇 단어를 읽는지 리딩 속도를 측정해보세요.

$$\frac{447 \ words}{reading \ time \ (\quad) \ sec} \times 60 = (\quad) \ WPM$$

Build Your Vocabulary

anxious [ǽŋkʃəs] a. 불안해하는, 염려하는; 열망하는 (**anxiously** ad. 근심하여, 걱정스럽게)
If you are anxious, you are nervous or worried about something.

rub [rʌb] v. (두 손 등을) 맞비비다; 문지르다; n. 문지르기, 비비기
If you rub two things together or if they rub together, they move backwards and forwards, pressing against each other.

pace [peis] v. 서성거리다; (일의) 속도를 유지하다; n. 속도; 걸음
If you pace a small area, you keep walking up and down it, because you are anxious or impatient.

back and forth idiom 앞뒤로; 좌우로; 여기저기에, 왔다 갔다
If someone moves back and forth, they repeatedly move in one direction and then in the opposite direction.

ranger [réindʒər] n. 삼림 관리원
A ranger is a person whose job is to look after a forest or large park.

staff [stæf] n. 직원; v. 직원으로 일하다
The staff of an organization are the people who work for it.

paleontologist [peiliəntálədʒist] n. 고생물학자
A paleontologist is a specialist in paleontology which is the earth science that studies fossil organisms and related remains.

복습 **nervous** [nə́:rvəs] a. 불안해하는, 초조해하는; 겁을 잘 먹는 (nervously ad. 초조하게)
If someone is nervous, they are frightened or worried about something
that is happening or might happen, and show this in their behavior.

복습 **nod** [nad] v. (고개를) 끄덕이다, 끄덕여 나타내다; n. (고개를) 끄덕임
If you nod, you move your head downward and upward to show
agreement, understanding, or approval.

복습 **fold** [fould] v. (두 손·팔 등을) 끼다; 접다; 감싸다; n. 주름; 접는 부분
If you fold your arms or hands, you bring them together and cross or
link them, for example over your chest.

복습 **sigh** [sai] v. 한숨을 쉬다, 한숨짓다; n. 한숨; 탄식
When you sigh, you let out a deep breath, as a way of expressing feelings
such as disappointment, tiredness, or pleasure.

복습 **fossil** [fásəl] n. 화석
A fossil is the hard remains of a prehistoric animal or plant that are found
inside a rock.

복습 **rare** [rɛər] a. 드문, 보기 힘든; 진귀한, 희귀한
Something that is rare is not common and is therefore interesting or
valuable.

in the first place idiom 우선, 먼저
You say in the first place when you are talking about the beginning of a
situation or about the situation as it was before a series of events.

복습 **please** [pli:z] v. 기쁘게 하다, 기분을 맞추다; ~하고 싶다; int. 부디, 제발
(pleased a. 기뻐하는, 만족해하는)
If you are pleased, you are happy about something or satisfied with
something

복습 **nightmare** [náitmɛər] n. 악몽; 아주 끔찍한 일
A nightmare is a very frightening dream.

go easy on idiom ~을 너그러이 봐주다; 살살 다루다
If you tell someone to go easy on, or be easy on, a particular person,
you are telling them not to punish or treat that person very severely.

unfortunately [ʌnfɔ́ːrʧənətli] ad. 불행하게도, 유감스럽게도
You can use unfortunately to introduce or refer to a statement when you consider that it is sad or disappointing, or when you want to express regret.

analysis [ənǽləsis] n. 분석; 분석 연구
Analysis is the scientific process of examining something in order to find out what it consists of.

rush [rʌʃ] v. 재촉하다; 급히 움직이다, 서두르다; n. 혼잡, 분주함; (감정이) 치밀어 오름
If you rush something, you do it in a hurry, often too quickly and without much care.

footprint [fútprint] n. (사람·동물의) 발자국
A footprint is a mark in the shape of a foot that a person or animal makes in or on a surface.

beam [biːm] v. 활짝 웃다; 비추다; n. 빛줄기; 환한 미소
If you say that someone is beaming, you mean that they have a big smile on their face because they are happy, pleased, or proud about something.

odds [adz] n. (어떤 일이 있을) 가능성; 역경, 곤란
You refer to how likely something is to happen as the odds that it will happen.

tool [tuːl] n. 도구, 연장; 수단
A tool is any instrument or simple piece of equipment that you hold in your hands and use to do a particular kind of work.

otherwise [ʌ́ðərwàiz] ad. 그렇지 않다면; 그 외에는; ~와는 다르게
You use otherwise after stating a situation or fact, in order to say what the result or consequence would be if this situation or fact was not the case.

display [displéi] n. 전시, 진열; v. 전시하다, 진열하다; 드러내다
A display is an arrangement of things that have been put in a particular place, so that people can see them easily.

case [keis] n. 용기, 통, 상자; 사례, 경우; 사건
A case is a container that is specially designed to hold or protect
something.

brass [bræs] n. 놋쇠, 황동
Brass is a yellow-colored metal made from copper and zinc.

plaque [plæk] n. (벽 등에 거는) 명판, 현판
A plaque is a flat piece of metal or stone with writing on it which is fixed
to a wall or other structure to remind people of an important person
or event.

dinosaur [dáinəsɔːr] n. 공룡
Dinosaurs were large reptiles which lived in prehistoric times.

discover [diskʌvər] v. 발견하다; 찾다, 알아내다
If a person or thing is discovered, someone finds them, either by accident
or because they have been looking for them.

nameplate [néimplèit] n. 명패, 명판; 문패
A nameplate is a piece of metal or plastic fastened onto something to
show who owns it, who has made it, or who lives or works there.

fancy [fǽnsi] a. 화려한; 값비싼; v. 생각하다, 상상하다; n. 공상, 상상
If you describe something as fancy, you mean that it is special, unusual,
or elaborate, for example because it has a lot of decoration.

pause [pɔːz] v. (말·일을 하다가) 잠시 멈추다; 정지시키다; n. 멈춤
If you pause while you are doing something, you stop for a short period
and then continue.

last [læst] v. 오래가다, 지속되다; 계속되다; 견디다
If something lasts for a particular length of time, it continues to be able
to be used for that time, for example because there is some of it left or
because it is in good enough condition.

page 5

"우리 도착했어!" 버스터가 소리쳤습니다.

랫번 선생님의 3학년 학급 나머지 학생들도 환호했습니다.

그들은 레인보우 록 주립 공원으로 들어가는 스쿨버스를 타고 있었습니다. 학급은 현장 학습을 위해 그곳에 왔습니다. 그 공원은 공룡을 포함하여 고대 동물들의 화석을 채집하기에 아주 좋은 곳이었습니다.

버스가 멈춰 서자, 랫번 선생님이 일어섰습니다.

"우리가 버스에서 내리면." 그가 말했습니다. "바깥에 질서정연하게 줄을 서렴."

page 6

아이들은 재빠르게 우르르 몰려나갔습니다. 질서정연하게라는 말을 그 누구도 신경 쓰지 않는 것 같았습니다.

빙키는 보도 위로 뛰어나갔습니다. 그는 허공에 대고 두 손을 허우적거렸습니다. "티. 렉스다. 으르렁!"

프랜신이 자기 머리를 그를 향해 낮추고 자신의 발을 굴렀습니다. "트리케라톱스. 어훙!"

버스터와 아서는 이러한 사나운 야수들 주위를 걸어갔습니다.

"난 우리가 여기에 왔다는 것이 믿기지 않아." 버스터가 말했습니다.

"나는 네가 계속 그렇게 말하는 것이 믿기지 않아." 아서가 말했습니다.

"뭐, 나는 흥분했을 뿐이야. 나는 시간, 분, 초를 세고 있었다고.... 정말 빨리 시작하고 싶어서 견딜 수가 없어."

버스터는 요즘 공룡에 대해 매우 관심이 많아졌습니다. 그는 도서관에서 책을 잔뜩 가져다 읽었고 비디오 가게에서 모든 공룡 영화를 보았습니다.

page 7

그리고 그는 오늘 특별히 준비를 해서 왔습니다. 다른 사람들이, 그들의 일반적인 옷을 입고 온 것과는 달리, 그는 아주 심혈을 기울여 옷을 입었습니다.

"그 모자 덥지 않아?" 아서가 물었습니다.

버스터가 고개를 저었습니다. "이건 모자가 아니야—피스 헬멧이라고. 이건 고생물학자들이 쓰는 거야. 그건 더운 사막 햇살로부터 그들을 시원하게 해줘."

아서는 주변을 돌아보았습니다. "음, 버스터, 네가 알아채지 못한 것 같은데, 우리는 지금 사막에 있지 않아."

버스터는 어깨를 들썩거렸습니다. "뭐, 난 잘 타거든. 그리고 무슨 일이 일어나든 준비가 된 것이 좋잖아. 예상하지 못한 것에 대비하라, 그게 나의 신조야." 그는 자신의 다용도 벨트를 가볍게 토닥거렸습니다. "그게 바로 우리가 이 모든 도구들을 가지고 온 이유이지."

"나에게 상기시키지 마." 아서가 말하면서, 그의 무거운 배낭을 다시 고쳐 매었습니다.

page 8

"넌 나중에 내게 고마워하게 될 거야. 우리는 허를 찔리고 싶지는 않으니까. 자, 우리가 끈은 어디에 두었지?"

"내가 가지고 있어." 아서가 말했습니다.

"휴대용 도감은?"

"그것도 가지고 있어."

"오! 우리가 그걸 잊은 건 아니었으면 좋겠는데—"

"걱정하지 마." 아서가 말하면서, 자신의 옆 주머니를 툭툭 쳤습니다. "내가 솔도 바로 여기에 가지고 있어."

랫번 선생님이 모두에게 주목하도록 했습니다. "잠깐만, 얘들아. 조용히 하렴."

학급 일부는 그를 향해 몸을 돌렸지만, 몇몇 아이들은 서로를 향해 계속 으르렁거리고 있었습니다.

"조용히 해!" 랫번 선생님이 소리쳤습니다.

page 10

으르렁거리는 소리가 멈추었습니다.

"고맙구나." 랫번 선생님이 침착하게 말했습니다. "여러분도 알겠지만, 우리는 공룡과 오래전 그들의 존재했다는 증거에 대해 더 배우기 위해 오늘 공원에 왔단다."

그는 빙키와 프랜신을 잠시 쳐다보았습니다. "모든 공룡들과 학생들은 자신들의 가장 좋은 태도를 보여야 할 거야. 알겠지?"

프랜신이 고개를 끄덕였습니다. 빙키는 그저 바닥을 내려다 보았습니다.

"훌륭해." 랫번 선생님이 말했습니다. "자 나를 따라오렴, 그럼 우리는 시작할 거야."

2장

page 11

랫번 선생님은 입구를 지나 작은 박물관으로 길을 안내했습니다. 첫 번째 방에는 뼈와 암석들을 전시하는 몇몇 유리 진열장들이 있었습니다. 한쪽 벽을 따라 브라키오사우루스와 하드로사우루스가 늪지에서 먹이를 먹고 있는 모습을 보여주는 입체 모형이 있었습니다.

"다른 것 없이 오직 샐러드만 하루 종일 먹는다면 난 질려버릴 거야." 프랜신이 말했습니다.

page 12

머피도 동의했습니다. "가장 좋은 수입 드레싱을 뿌린다고 해도, 그건 꽤 질리겠지."

랫번 선생님은 그를 기다리는 것으로

보이는 삼림 관리원에게 다가갔습니다. 그들은 악수를 하고 인사를 나누었습니다.

"학급 여러분, 이 분은 루스 대원이란 다." 랫번 선생님이 알렸습니다. "우리가 나가서 직접 답사를 해보기 전에 루스 대원께서 우리에게 화석에 대해 몇 가지 알려주실 거야."

루스 대원이 학급을 향해 상냥하게 미소 지었습니다. "안녕, 얘들아! 세상에, 정말 똑똑해 보이는 남자 여자아이들이구나! 화석이 무엇인지 말해줄 사람?"

몇몇 아이들이 눈을 굴렸습니다.

버스터가 손을 들었습니다.

"오, 좋아. 지원자. 자, 수줍어하지 말고. 화석이 뭐라고 생각하니?"

버스터가 깊게 숨을 들이마셨습니다. "화석이란 고대 유기체들의 석회화된 잔여물입니다. 광물질이 유기체의 조직 속으로 스며들어서 고체화되어, 그것들의 본래 모양을 보존하게 되는 것입니다."

page 13

"이런, 이런, 이런!" 루스 대원은 깜짝 놀라 보였습니다. "학급 천재를 선발하는 것을 나에게 맡기면 잘 할 수 있겠는데. 바로 이동하면, 여러분에게 보여줄 작은 공연이 있어요. 조명!"

방 안에 조명이 흐려지자, 공룡 입체 모형에 스포트라이트가 비쳤습니다.

루스 대원은 마이크에 대고 말했습니다. "1억 년 전에, 레인보우 록 주립 공원은 아주 다르게 보였답니다. 훨씬 더 더웠지요. 그리고 양치식물들이 많았어요."

그때, 양치식물처럼 옷을 입은 대원이 느릿느릿 시야에 나타났습니다.

"또 곤충들도 아주 많았지요." 루스 대원이 계속 이어나갔습니다.

또 다른 대원이 잠자리처럼 옷을 입고서, 무대 위로 파닥거리며 올라왔습니다.

"으웩!" 학급이 같이 말했습니다.

"그리고, 물론, 공룡도 있었지요."

아이들은 환호했습니다.

page 14

브라키오사우루스 옷 안에 들어간 삼림 관리원 두 명이 무대 위로 뒤뚱거리며 올라왔습니다.

"결국, 양치식물들과 동물들은 죽었습니다."

양치식물 의상을 입은 사람이 바닥에 털썩 쓰러졌습니다.

아이들이 키득거렸습니다.

그러더니 잠자리도 쓰러졌고, 브라키오사우루스는 반으로 갈라져, 앞부분은 무대 위에 남아있는 반면에 뒷부분은 도망쳐 버렸습니다.

모두 웃었습니다.

"조용히 하렴!" 랫번 선생님이 말했습니다.

"고마워요." 루스 대원이 말했습니다. "자, 보통 몸체는 썩어 없어져요. 그러나 때때로, 껍데기나 뼈와 같은, 몸체의 딱딱한 부분은 남아있게 되지요."

브라키오사우루스 앞부분이 그 의상의 지퍼를 열어, 그 아래에 있던 브라키오사우루스 골격 의상을 드러냈습니다.

"무척이나 오랜 시간이 흐른 뒤, 이 모든 지역은 바다로 뒤덮였습니다. 수백만 년이 넘는 시간 동안, 흙은 암석으로 변했어요. 그리고 뼈와 껍데기도 또한, 암석으로 변했지요."

page 16

조명이 희미해지면서, 파도가 부딪치는 소리가 확성기를 통해 나왔습니다.

"그리고 나서 바다가 말랐어요. 그리고 마침내, 또 1억 년이 지난 후에, 오늘에 이르렀습니다."

스포트라이트가 켜지며, 전시실의 저편에 있는 커다란 브라키오사우루스 골격을 보여주었습니다.

불이 다시 켜지자, 아이들은 손뼉을 쳤습니다.

"자." 루스 대원이 말했습니다. "화석 채집을 가고 싶은 사람?"

3장

page 17

학급은 높은 세일 절벽으로 둘러싸인 골짜기를 지나서 루스 대원을 뒤따라 걸어갔습니다. 모든 사람은 들통과 삽을 들고 있었습니다.

"난 너무 흥분돼!" 버스터가 아서에게 말했습니다.

"정말? 나는 전혀 예상하지 못했는걸."

"나는 그 화석들 가운데 하나를 내 손에 넣는 게 정말 기대돼." 버스터가 계속 말했습니다. "내 말은, 이건 진짜잖아. 수백만 년 전에 살았던 무언가의 진짜 흔적이라고."

"주목하세요!" 루스 대원이 말했습니다. "잘 들어 보렴!"

page 18

학급은 한 절벽 앞에 멈춰 섰습니다. 흙과 바위의 층들이 절벽에 다른 색의 줄무늬를 만들어냈습니다.

"이 암석에 있는 층들이 보이니?" 루스 대원이 계속 말했습니다. "각 층은 다른 시기에 만들어졌어. 가장 밑에 있는 것은 백악기 초기, 대략 1억 3천5백만 년 전에 만들어진 것이지."

"와." 빙키가 말했습니다. "그건 심지어 TV가 만들어지기도 전이잖아."

"자, 맨 위에 있는 층은 2천만 년 후에 만들어진 것이야." 대원은 계속 말했습니다. "그래서 우리는 화석이 얼마나 오래되었는지를 그것이 절벽의 어떤 위치에서 나왔는지 확인해보면 알 수 있단다."

머피는 혼란스러워 보였습니다. "어떻게 우리가 절벽에서 화석을 꺼낼 수 있겠어요?" 그녀가 물었습니다. "우리가 가진 건 이 조그만 통이 전부잖아요."

page 19

"걱정하지 않아도 된단다." 루스 대원이 말했습니다. "절벽은 전문 고생물학자들을 위한 것이야. 너희는 개울에서 채집할 거란다."

"개울에서요?" 프랜신이 말했습니다. "좋아요!"

그녀는 물로 뛰어들어서 여기저기에서 첨벙거리기 시작했습니다.

"물이 좋은데." 그녀가 소리쳤습니다. "어, 이것 봐, 나 화석을 찾았어! 어, 아니, 잠시만. 이건 돌이네. 얘, 여기 또 하나 있어!"

아이들 모두 곧 그녀를 따라서 들어갔습니다.

랫번 선생님은 걸어 다니며, 격려의 말을 했습니다. 그가 아서와 버스터에게 다가갔을 때, 그는 보기 위해 멈추었습니다. 버스터는 위아래로 급하게 움직이면서, 정신없이 화석을 찾고 있었습니다.

"뭐 좀 찾았니, 얘들아?"

"아니요!" 그들이 함께 대답했습니다.

"오. 그래, 우리는 이제 간식을 먹기 위해 잠시 쉴 거야, 그리고 나면 우리는 다시 버스로 돌아갈 거란다."

page 20

아서는 몸을 똑바르게 세웠습니다. "뭐." 그가 말하면서, 기지개를 켰습니다. "이제 끝난 것 같은데."

"난 아주 마지막 순간까지 멈추지 않을 거야." 버스터가 말했습니다.

아서는 랫번 선생님과 대원을 바라보았습니다. 그들은 아이스박스에서 주스와 쿠키를 꺼내고 있었습니다.

"버스터! 나 먹을 것이 보여! 그리고 마실 것도!"

"난 관심 없어." 버스터가 말했습니다. "우리는 언제든지 간식을 먹을 수 있잖아. 여기에 화석들이 있다고!"

"너 정말 괜찮은 거 맞니, 버스터? 난 네가 전에 음식을 거절하는 것을 본 적이 없어."

"응, 난 괜찮아. 난 훨씬 더 괜찮아."

"어서, 그럼." 아서가 말했습니다. "단지 몇 분 더 있다고 해서 네가 뭘 찾을 수 있을 거라고 기대하는 거야? 네가 그냥 안으로 손을 뻗어서 뭔가를 찾아낼 수는 없는 거라고!"

page 21

아서는 물속으로 손을 뻗었고 무늬가 있는 돌을 꺼내 들었습니다.

버스터는 화가 나서 그를 향해 몸을 돌렸습니다. 그러더니 아서가 그의 손에 들고 있는 것을 그가 보았을 때 그의 표정이 멍해졌습니다.

"버스터? 너 괜찮니?"

버스터가 그를 향해 천천히 다가오기 시작했습니다. 그의 두 손은 쭉 뻗어 있었습니다.

아서가 뒤로 물러났습니다. "버스터? 그만둬! 너 나를 불안하게 하고 있단 말이야."

아서가 그 돌을 떨어뜨렸습니다.

"아아아아아아!" 버스터가 말했습니다.

그는 그 특별한 돌이 떨어진 자리로 뛰어들었고 그가 찾을 수 있는 아무 돌이나 집어 들기 시작했습니다. 그는 하나씩 힐끗 보고는, 던져 버렸습니다.

"버스터, 너 미쳤니?"

버스터가 다른 돌을 하나 집어 들더니, 그것도 역시, 거의 집어 던질 뻔하다가, 그러더니 자신의 가슴에 와락 움켜쥐었습니다.

page 23

"찾았어! 내가 찾았다고!"

아서가 보려고 다가왔습니다. "뭘 찾았다는 거야?" 그가 물었습니다. "나 좀 보여줘."

버스터가 그렇게 했습니다. 그 돌은 세 갈래의 자국이 새겨져 있었습니다.

"오, 와." 아서가 말했습니다. "이건 나뭇잎 화석이네."

"나뭇잎 화석이라고? 나뭇잎 화석이라니, 그게 무슨 말이야? 너 이렇게 두꺼운 나뭇잎 본 적 있어?"

버스터가 그것을 빛을 향해 들어 올렸습니다. 그는 깊은숨을 들이마셨습니다. "아서." 그가 말했습니다. "이건 발자국이야."

page 24

다른 아이들이 간식을 먹고 있는 동안에, 버스터는 한 손으로 그의 주머니를 꽉 움켜쥔 채 앉아 있었습니다.

"버스터, 너 쿠키 좀 먹을래?" 아서가 물었습니다.

버스터가 고개를 저었습니다.

"주스는 좀 어때?"

버스터가 또 고개를 저었습니다. 그는 뭔가를 먹거나 마시기에는 너무 흥분한 상태였습니다. 그는 그냥 숨을 쉬는 것조차도 매우 버거웠습니다. 상상해보세요! 그가 진짜 공룡 화석을 발견한 것입니다. 그는 지금 신문 헤드라인을 그려 볼 수 있었습니다: **버스터 백스터의 큰 행운.** 세계 곳곳에서 온 고생물학자들이 단지 그와 악수를 하려고 줄을 설 것입니다.

루스 대원은 자기 셔츠에 묻은 쿠키 부스러기를 털어냈습니다. "내가 보기엔 모두 식욕이 왕성한 것 같은데." 그녀가 말했습니다. "마저 먹을 동안, 우리가 찾은 화석에 대해 돌아가면서 이야기해 볼까."

알렉스와 브레인이 중심에서부터 홈이 퍼져나가는 회색 돌을 집어 올렸습니다.

"우리가 생각하기엔 이건 아마 껍데기였던 것 같아요." 브레인이 말했습니다.

루스 대원은 그 돌을 집어 살펴봤습니다. "아주 좋아. 그리고 그냥 아무 껍데기가 아니야. 삿갓조개인 것 같구나."

그녀는 그것을 상자에 넣었습니다.

알렉스와 브레인은 기뻐 보였습니다. "그건 전시가 될까요?" 브레인이 물었습니다.

"지켜보자구나." 대원이 말했습니다. "나 말고도 많은 사람들이 그 결정을 함께 내리거든."

버스터가 눈을 깜빡였습니다. "잠깐만요!" 그가 소리쳤습니다. "우리가 찾은 것을 가질 수는 없나요?"

루스 대원이 고개를 저었습니다. "오, 유감이야. 아마 내가 아까 설명했을 때 넌 듣지 않은 모양이구나. 우리는 박물관에 가능한 많은 화석들을 두어서 모든 사람이 그것들을 볼 기회를 가질 수 있게 하려고 한단다."

"그리고 제대로 출처를 넣어주겠지요." 브레인이 말했습니다.

"물론이지." 대원이 말했습니다. "우리는 화석을 찾은 사람이라면 누구에게나 그 공을 인정한단다."

그녀는 버스터를 향해 미소 지었습니다. "알겠니?"

"네, 그런 것 같아요." 버스터가 다시 자리에 앉았습니다. "믿을 수 없어." 그가 혼잣말로 중얼거렸습니다. "어떻게 그들이 나한테 이럴 수가 있지?"

프랜신은 돌 몇 개를 집어 들었습니다. "이것들을 봐주세요. 전 여기에 아무 화석도 없는 것 같아요. 하지만 그 돌들은 여전히 꽤 신기해요."

대원이 그것들을 검토했습니다. "응, 그렇구나. 운모와 석영의 줄무늬인 것 같네, 내가 생각하기에는 말이야. 좀 더 연구하기 위해 내가 그것들을 갖고 있을게."

프랜신이 활짝 웃었습니다. "그것 봐." 그녀가 머피에게 말했습니다. "좀 더 연구해본대. 난 중요한 돌을 찾은 거야."

머피는 어깨를 으쓱했습니다. "유일하게 정말 중요한 돌들은 반지나 목걸이에 박혀 있는 것들뿐이지."

"또 다른 사람은 없니?" 루스 대원이 말했습니다.

몇몇 다른 아이들이 그녀에게 그들이 찾은 것들을 보여주었습니다.

아서가 버스터의 옆구리를 찔렀습니다.

"그만해!" 버스터가 속삭였습니다.

"하지만... 하지만...." 아서가 말하기 시작했습니다.

"너희는 뭔가 추가할 게 있니?" 대원이 물었습니다. "우리의 떠오르는 전문가는 보여주고 싶은 뭔가를 찾았니?"

"없어요." 버스터가 말했습니다. "전혀 없어요."

아서는 놀란 듯 보였습니다. "무슨 말이야?" 그가 속삭였습니다. "난 우리가—"

page 29

버스터가 아서의 갈비뼈를 팔꿈치로 찔렀습니다. "괜찮아요." 그가 루스 대원에게 말했습니다. "우리가 아무것도 보여드릴 게 없어서 아서가 조금 쑥스러운 모양이에요."

대원이 아서의 등을 토닥거렸습니다. "걱정하지 마, 아서. 과학자로서, 우리는 인내심을 배워야 한단다. 난 네가 다음에 뭔가를 찾을 수 있다고 확신해."

"그렇겠죠." 아서가 말하면서, 버스터를 험악하게 힐끗 쳐다보았습니다. "벌써 기분이 조금 나아졌네요."

5장

page 30

그들이 떠나기 전에 아이들에게는 놀 시간이 조금 남아있었습니다. 빙키는 다시 *티렉스*가 되어, 지나가는 모든 사람에게 으르렁거리고 발톱을 치켜세우는 시늉을 했습니다. 프랜신과 머피는 먹이를 찾는 익룡처럼 잔디 위로 뛰어들었습니다.

아서는 공룡 놀이를 할 기분이 아니었습니다. 그는 불안했습니다.

"우리는 절대 이걸 가지고 무사히 빠져나가지 못할 거야." 그들이 피크닉 테이블에 앉아있는 동안에, 그가 버스터에게 조용히 말했습니다.

page 31

"두고 보자고." 버스터가 말했습니다.

"그렇지만 화석은 우리 것이 아니잖아—내 말은, 네 것이 아니라고. 무슨 말이냐면, 너는 이걸 찾은 것을 인정받아야 하지만, 이건 박물관에 있어야만 한단 말이야."

"난 그걸 포기하지 않을 거야." 버스터가 말했습니다. 그는 화석을 부드럽게 움켜쥐었습니다. "이건 마치 역사의 일부를 잡고 있는 것과 같다고."

"그렇지만 만약 그들이 나가는 길에 우리를 수색하면 어떡해? 우리는 체포될지도 몰라! 만약 그들이 특별한 화석-감지 경보장치를 갖고 있으면 어떡 할 거냐고?"

"난 그런 것에 대해선 들어본 적 없 어."

"글쎄, 그건 전혀 내 기분을 나아지게 하지 않아." 아서가 말했습니다. "기억하 니, 교실에 머피가 염소 치즈를 갖고 왔 고 넌 그게 가짜라고 주장했을 때—네 가 그런 것에 대해 들어본 적이 없었다 는 이유로 말이야?"

"그건 다른 경우지." 버스터가 말했 습니다. "만약에 염소들이 먹는 것이라 고는 통조림밖에 없다면 그들이 치즈 를 만들어낼 수 있다는 건 말이 안 된다 고."

page 32

"글쎄, 너는 그렇지 않다는 걸 알게 되었잖아, 그렇지 않니? 그리고 과학자 들이 엑스레이 레이저를 발명해냈던 바 이오닉 버니 에피소드는 어떻고? 그런 것들 가운데 하나쯤은 여기에 있을 수 도 있어."

아서는 불안한 기색으로 주변을 둘러 보았습니다.

"그렇지만, 바이오닉 버니는 텔레비전 프로그램이잖아." 버스터가 말했습니 다.

"알아. 그런데 거기에 나오는 많은 내 용들이 아주 현실적이지. 실화에 기초 한 것 같아, 내가 생각하기에는."

"아마 그럴지도 모르지." 버스터가 말 했습니다. "하지만 난 그렇게 생각하지 않아—"

휘이이잇!

랫번 선생님이 자신의 호루라기를 불 고 있었습니다.

"자, 얘들아." 그가 소리쳤습니다. "모 두 모이렴. 버스가 왔어. 혹시 두고 가 는 물건이 없는지 소지품을 확인해라."

버스터는 자신의 주머니 위로 다시 자 기 손을 얹었습니다. 화석은 안전했습 니다. 그의 손가락으로 발자국의 투박 한 윤곽을 느낄 수 있었습니다.

page 33

"이런." 아서가 말했습니다. "봐, 버스 터, 루스 대원이 우리에게 다가오고 있 어. 그녀가 우리를 몸수색할 거야. 내가 이런 일이 일어날 거라고 말했지. 하지 만 넌 들으려고 했니? 아니이이이이. 그 들은 나무 안에 일종의 감지기를 숨겨 놓은 것이 틀림없어. 아마 그건 적외선 으로 작동하는—"

"쉬이이이잇!" 버스터가 쉿 소리를 냈 습니다.

루스 대원이 버스터 바로 앞으로 와 서 멈췄습니다.

"마지막으로 내게 묻고 싶은 게 있 니?" 그녀가 말했습니다.

"음, 없는 것 같은데요."

루스 대원이 웃었습니다. "음, 아마 대

신 나에게 말하고 싶은 것이 있을 것 같은데."

"어떤 거요?"

"글쎄, 잘 모르겠어. 공룡에 대한 새로운 사실일 수도 있지. 아니면..."

아서는 그의 두 눈을 질끈 감았습니다. 올 것이 오고야 말았습니다. 감마선 감지망이 그들은 잡아낸 것이 틀림없었습니다. 그들은 가망이 없었습니다.

"... 너희가 좋은 시간을 보냈다고 말해줄 수도 있겠지."

버스터는 갑자기 밝아졌습니다. "오, 맞아요."

"넌 조금 불편해 보이는구나." 대원이 말했습니다. 그녀는 버스터의 등을 토닥거렸습니다. "난 네가 화석 채집 때문에 너무 의기소침하지 말았으면 좋겠구나. 너는 진짜 고생물학자가 될 자질이 있어."

"감사합니다."

그녀는 랫번 선생님에게 작별 인사를 하려고 갔습니다.

"봤지?" 버스터가 말했습니다. "우리는 완전히 안전해."

"아마 지금은 그럴지도." 아서는 말했습니다.

6장

page 36

방과 후에, 아서는 프랜신과 브레인에게 화석에 대해 말하고 싶었지만, 버스터가 그것을 허락하지 않았습니다.

"너무 위험해." 그가 설명했습니다.

"뭐, 우리가 누구한테 말할 수 있니?" 아서가 물었습니다.

"아무한테도. 우리는 그것을 비밀로 해야만 해."

버스터가 집에 갔을 때, 그는 자신의 방으로 곧장 들어갔습니다. 그는 문을 닫았고 창문 블라인드를 내렸습니다.

"방어선 보안 가동 중." 그가 말했습니다.

다음으로, 그는 은박지로 화석을 포장했습니다. 그러더니 그는 그것을 비닐봉지 안에 담았고 그 봉지를 신발 상자 안에 넣었습니다.

page 37

"1단계 완료."

그는 신발 상자의 나머지 부분을 그릇에 있던 구슬로 채웠고 그것을 그의 옷장 안 선반 위에 올려놓았습니다.

"2단계 완료." 그가 말했습니다. "보안 체계 설정. 경계 태세 확인."

그의 어머니와 할머니와 함께하는 저녁 식사 자리에서, 버스터는 말이 없었습니다.

"너 괜찮은 거니?" 그의 어머니가 물었습니다. "너 너무 조용하구나."

"그냥 좀 피곤한 것 같아요." 버스터가 말했습니다.

"현장 학습은 어땠니?"

"괜찮았어요." 버스터가 말했습니다.

"뭐 좋은 화석이라도 찾았니?"

버스터는 하마터면 우유를 쏟을 뻔했습니다.

"화석이요? 뭐 때문에 그걸 물으시는 거예요?"

"글쎄, 버스터. 난 그 때문에 네가 공원에 갔다고 생각했는데."

page 39

"아, 맞아요. 음, 꽤 흥미로웠어요. 공연도 있었고요. 대원이 친절했어요. 그리고 우리는 여기저기 걸어 다닐 수도 있었어요."

그의 엄마는 고개를 끄덕였습니다. "네가 좋았다니 기쁘구나."

"내가 네 나이 때는 말이다." 버스터의 할머니가 말했습니다. "우리는 화석을 채집하러 가지 않았어." 그녀가 잠시 멈추었습니다. "그때는 말이지, 공룡들이 아직 살아 있었지. 그렇고말고."

버스터의 어머니가 웃었습니다.

버스터는 그저 눈을 굴렸습니다.

"너 매시 포테이토에 지금 뭘 한 거니?" 그의 엄마가 물었습니다.

버스터는 자신의 접시를 내려다보았

습니다.

"그건 마치 공룡 발자국처럼 보이는구나." 그의 엄마가 계속 말했습니다.

"아니에요, 아니에요." 버스터가 말하면서, 한 입을 떴고 그것을 삼켰습니다. "그저 무늬일 뿐이에요. 그게 다예요."

page 40

잠시 뒤, 버스터는 잠자리에 들기 위해 자기 방으로 올라왔습니다. 마침내 잠이 들기 전까지 그는 오랫동안 뒤척였습니다.

콰앙! 쾅!

"저 소리는 뭐지?" 버스터는 궁금했습니다. 그는 창문 밖을 내다보았습니다.

커다란 공룡이 그를 마주 보고 있었습니다.

"너 여기 있었구나!" 공룡이 말했습니다.

"누구, 나?" 버스터가 말했습니다.

"그래, 너—내 발자국을 가져간 소년. 다시 돌려줘—당장!"

"내가 생각하기엔 너는 지금 나를 다른 사람과 혼동하는 것 같은데." 버스터가 말했습니다.

"아니야, 그렇지 않아." 공룡이 말했습니다. "아마도 넌 내가 그렇게 크지 않다고 나를 무시해도 된다고 생각할지 모르지. 바보 같지 굴지 마. 난 크고 힘센 친구들이 있다고."

공룡은 자신의 뒤로 꼬리를 홱 흔들었습니다. 버스터는 티라노사우루스와 트리케라톱스가 그곳에 서 있는 것을 보았습니다. 티라노사우루스는, 그런데, 빙키의 머리가 달렸고, 트리케라톱스는 프랜신의 머리가 달려 있었습니다.

page 41

"발자국을 돌려줘!" 그들이 소리쳤습니다.

"절대 안 돼!" 버스터가 말했고, 그는 창문을 쾅 닫았습니다.

그는 무엇을 해야 할까요? 그들은 무엇을 하려는 것일까요?

갑자기 방이 흔들리기 시작했습니다. 선반에서 책들이 떨어졌고, 색연필이 담긴 상자가 바닥으로 쏟아졌습니다.

"우리가 간다!" 밖에서 목소리가 말했습니다. "우리는 발자국을 원해!"

버스터는 화석이 들어 있는 신발 상자를 잡고 그것을 꽉 안았습니다.

방이 그의 주변에서 흔들렸고, 그는 끝나기를 기다렸습니다.

7장

page 42

"와!" 아서가 말했습니다. "그거 정말 대단한 꿈인데."

다음 날 아침 그와 버스터는 수업이 시작하기 전에 책상 앞에 앉아있었습니다. 버스터는 자기 악몽의 세세한 부분들을 이야기하고 있었습니다.

"가장 최악이었던 것은." 버스터가 말했습니다. "빙키의 머리가 티라노사우루스 위에 놓인 것이 너무 자연스러워 보였다는 거야."

"프랜신의 머리는 어땠어?"

버스터가 웃었습니다. 그는 교실의 다른 쪽에서 머피와 수 엘렌에게 이야기하고 있는 프랜신을 보았습니다. "그녀는 절대 완전히 정상으로 보인 적이 없었으니까." 그가 말했습니다.

page 43

아서가 고개를 끄덕였습니다. 그는 버스터가 그 꿈에 대해 이야기해준 것이 기뻤지만, 자신이 그 꿈을 꾸지 않았다는 것에 더욱 기뻤습니다.

"적어도 이제 끝난 일이잖아." 버스터가 말했습니다.

"맞아." 아서가 말했습니다. "그렇지만 네 꿈이 네게 뭔가를 말하려고 한다고 생각하지 않니?"

버스터는 곰곰이 생각해보았습니다.

"응, 그건 내 애플파이 위에 초콜릿 소스를 너무 많이 치지 말라고 말하고 있어. 난 잠자기 전에 배가 약간 아팠던 것 같아."

아서는 한숨 쉬었습니다. "그래서 내가 언제 놀러 가서 그걸 볼 수 있을까?"

"안 돼, 아무도 안 돼."

아서는 놀라 보였습니다. "왜 안 되는데?"

"난 매우 세심한 보안 태세를 갖추어 놓았다고. 그것은 건드리지 않는 게 좋아."

"내가 조심할게." 아서가 주장했습니다.

"미안해. 너무 위험해. 만약 엄마가 들어오면 어떡해?"

"하지만 버스터, 우리가 그걸 보지도 못한다면 이름을—말하면—안 되는—그것을 가지고 있는 게 무슨 의미가 있겠니?"

page 44

버스터는 프랜신이 다가오고 있었기 때문에 그 질문에 답을 해야 하는 것을 피할 수 있었습니다.

"좋은 아침이야, 아서. 넌 조금 피곤해 보이는구나, 버스터. 잠을 잘 자지 못했구나, 응? 아마 어제 네가 아무것도 찾지 못해서 기분이 안 좋은가 봐."

"무슨 말이니?"

"내 말은 공원에서 말이야. 너는 대단한 전문가잖아, 고생물학자 씨."

버스터의 얼굴이 빨개졌습니다. "내가 화석을 좋아한다는 것은 사실이지."

"그런데 너의 모든 지식, 네 모든 도구들... 그리고, 그래, 네 모자도 잊으면 안 되지—"

"피스 헬멧이야." 버스터가 그녀의 말을 고쳐주었습니다.

"피스 헬멧." 프랜신이 따라 했습니다. "심지어 그 모든 걸 갖고서도, 넌 아무것도 찾지 못했잖아."

page 45

버스터는 조용했습니다.

"프랜신, 너는 공정하게 굴지 않고 있어." 아서가 말했습니다. "버스터는 어제 찾는 일을 아주 잘해냈어." 아서는 프랜신을 노려보았습니다. "정말 잘했단 말이야."

그녀는 그저 웃었습니다.

"잠시만." 랫번 선생님이 말했습니다. "모두 자리에 앉으렴."

반 전체가 자리에 앉았을 때, 그가 말을 계속했습니다.

"너희 모두 어제 우리의 현장학습을 즐겼다면 좋겠구나. 진짜 화석을 찾을 기회를 가져서 재미있었을 거라고 생각한단다. 물론, 찾는 건 쉽지 않았지. 만약 우리가 어떤 공룡 뼈나 이빨의 흔적을 찾았다면 정말 놀라웠을 거야."

아서가 약간 꼼지락거리는 동안에 버스터는 두 손으로 그의 입으로 막았고 자기 눈을 자신의 긴 귀로 가렸습니다.

"아니면, 훨씬 더 희귀한, 공룡 발자국이라든지 말이야. 그랬다면 정말 신나지 않았겠니?"

모두 고개를 끄덕였습니다.

page 47

랫번 선생님이 어깨를 으쓱했습니다. "하지만 이번에는 그런 일이 일어나지 않았지. 뭐라고 했니, 버스터?"

"아무것도 아니에요, 랫번 선생님."

"아. 난 네가 신음하는 소리를 들은 줄 알았단다. 흠, 아무튼, 역사를 통틀어 훌륭한 과학자들은 처음에는 실망하지만 나중에는 성공한다는 것을 기억하렴."

버스터는 그의 책상 위에 털썩 앞으로 쓰러졌습니다. 이 비밀을 지키는 것은 그가 생각했던 것보다 점점 더 힘들어지고 있었습니다.

8장

page 48

백스터 부인은 걱정되었습니다.

"괜찮니, 애야?" 그녀가 물었습니다.

버스터는 그의 침대에서 펄쩍 뛰었습니다. "괜찮으냐고요? 물론이에요, 괜찮아요. 제가 왜 괜찮지 않겠어요? 저 괜찮아 보이지 않나요?"

그의 엄마는 확신할 수 없었습니다. "음, 넌 조금 피곤해 보이는구나. 학교에서 무슨 문제가 있는 건 아니겠지, 그렇지?"

"아니에요, 아니에요." 버스터가 말했습니다. "학교에서는 다 좋아요."

전화가 울렸습니다.

버스터가 뛰어가서 받았습니다.

page 49

"여보세요?"

"안녕." 아서가 말했습니다. "난 우리 수학 숙제에 대해서 질문이 있어. 우리 물건을 피트로 측정해야 해, 아니면 *미터*로 재야 해?"

"피트(*foot*)? 왜 너는 발(*foot*)이라고 말하는 거니?"

"그럼 내가 달리 어떻게 말하니?" 아서가 물었다.

"날 속이지 마." 버스터가 말했습니다. "넌 우리가 두 가지 방법을 다 써야 한다는 것을 완벽하게 잘 알고 있잖아. 너는 그저 내 이름을—말하면—안 되는 것에 대해 확인하려는 거야."

"솔직히, 버스터, 난 기억이 나지 않았—"

"그래, 그래, 좋은 시도였어, 아서. 내일 보자. 안녕."

그는 전화를 끊고 방으로 돌아왔습니다.

그는 그의 엄마가 신발 상자를 들고 있는 것을 보았습니다.

"이게 뭐니, 버스터? 이거 꽤 무겁구나."

"그거요?" 버스터가 재빨리 달려갔고 그녀의 손에서 그것을 뺏었습니다. "이거 학교 과제예요. 아주 까다롭죠. 쉬쉬하고 있죠. 극비예요. 이것에 대해 말씀드릴 수 없어요."

page 50

그는 그것을 옷장 안에 다시 집어넣었습니다.

엄마는 걱정스러워 보였습니다. "넌 좀 쉬어야겠구나, 얘야. 아마 일찍 잠자리에 드는 게 좋겠어."

버스터는 창문을 힐끗 보았습니다. "잠자리에? 일찍이요?" 그는 낄낄거리듯 말했습니다. "그게 좋겠네요."

잠시 후, 버스터는 침대에 누워서, 화석에 대해 생각하고 있었습니다. 그의 눈꺼풀이 아래로 쳐지기 시작했습니다.

문에서 두드리는 소리가 들렸습니다.

"누구세요?" 버스터가 물었습니다.

"화석 경찰입니다."

"네?" 버스터가 말했습니다.

문이 활짝 열렸습니다. 루스 대원과 경찰이 들어왔습니다. 그들은 자신들의 뒤로 아서를 끌고 오고 있었습니다. 그는 줄무늬가 있는 죄수복을 입고 있었습니다.

"미안해, 버스터." 아서가 말했습니다. "그들이 내가 말하도록 했어. 그들이 나를 간지럽혔어."

page 51

"왜 너는 스스로를 방어하지 않았니?" 버스터가 물었습니다.

아서가 자신의 팔을 들어 올렸습니다. 그는 수갑을 차고 있었습니다.

"아름다운 장면은 아니구나, 그렇지?" 루스 대원이 말했습니다. "너에게도 똑같은 처치가 준비되어 있단다."

"저요?" 버스터가 말했습니다. "제가 뭘 했는데요?"

대원은 웃었습니다. "우리는 네가 이 방에 공룡을 숨기고 있다고 믿을 만한 이유가 있단다."

버스터의 눈길이 자기 옷장으로 힐끗 향했습니다. "그렇지만 그건 말도 안 돼요! 수백만 년 동안 공룡은 없었다고요. 어떻게—"

루스 대원과 경찰은 그의 옷장으로 향한 버스터의 시선을 따라갔습니다. 그러더니 그들은 이상한 소리를 듣고 멈춰 섰습니다.

쿵, 쿵, 쿵

"이것에 대해 설명해볼래, 고생물학자 씨?" 루스 대원이 물었습니다.

page 53

"무엇을 설명하라는 거죠?" 버스터가 말했습니다. "저는 아무것도 들리지 않는데요."

쿵, 쿵, 쿵

"물러서세요." 대원이 말했습니다. "우리는 지금—"

갑자기 옷장 문이 벌컥 열렸습니다. 티라노사우루스 렉스가 걸어 나오면서,

그들을 향해 포효했습니다.

"잘못을 인정하네요." 대원이 말했습니다.

"그는 배고파 보여요." 아서가 말했습니다.

"걱정하지 마." 대원이 말했습니다. "우리는 매우 안전하니까. 그는 단지 버스터가 그를 옷장에 가둬서 화가 났을 뿐이야."

티라노사우루스는 그의 입을 넓게 벌리면서, 자신의 이빨을 전부 다 보여줬습니다.

버스터가 비명을 질렀습니다.

9장

page 54

버스터는 다음 날 학교에 결석했습니다. 아서는 버스터가 그저 아픈 것이라고 생각했기 때문에 그렇게 걱정하지 않았습니다. 그러나 그는 집에 가는 길에 백스터 가족의 아파트에 들르기로 했습니다.

백스터 부인이 그를 안으로 들였습니다.

"안녕, 아서. 잘 지내니?"

"잘 지내요."

백스터 부인은 한숨을 쉬었습니다. "버스터도 그렇다고 말할 수 있었으면 좋겠구나. 그 애가 어젯밤에 잠을 잘 자지 못해서 난 오늘 그냥 그를 집에 있게 했단다. 그래도, 그가 아프거나 전염병이 있는 것 같지는 않으니, 가서 그를 만나보렴.

page 55

"감사합니다, 백스터 부인."

아서가 버스터의 방에 다다랐을 때, 그는 문이 닫혀있는 걸 확인했습니다. 그는 문을 두드렸습니다.

"버스터! 나야, 아서."

버스터가 문을 열었습니다. 그는 아직도 파자마를 입고 있었습니다.

"너 마침 잘 왔어, 아서. 나는 마지막 준비를 위한 도움이 필요해."

아서가 눈을 깜빡였습니다. 방은 난장판이었습니다. 모든 것이 옷장에서 꺼내져 나와 있었고, 줄로 만들어진 망이 십자 모양으로 방을 가로지르고 있었습니다.

"너 뭐 하니?" 아서가 물었습니다.

"음, 우선 나는 옷장을 비웠어. 이렇게 해서 한눈에 안에 뭐가 있는지 볼 수 있게 말이야. 나는 어떤 공룡도 그 안에 숨지 않았으면 하거든." 그는 줄을 가리켰습니다. "그리고 이제 나는 공룡 탐지기를 만들고 있어. 공룡이 오면, 그들은 불시에 나를 공격하지는 못할 거야."

"하지만 버스터, 공룡은 수억 년 동안 멸종 상태였어. 너도 알고 있잖아."

page 56

"난 그것이 단지 우리가 그렇게 믿도록 그들이 바라는 것이라고 생각해. 그 모든 게 그들의 종합 계획 가운데 일부란 말이야."

"그들의 종합 계획이라고?"

버스터가 고개를 끄덕였습니다. "그게 바로 그들이 그 모든 화석이 발견되도록 남겨둔 이유야. 그들은 우리를 속이고 싶은 거야. 하지만 난 속지 않아. 난 준비되어 있을 거야."

아서가 침대 위에 앉았습니다.

"네가 지금 살짝 극단적이라고 생각하지 않니?"

버스터가 코웃음을 쳤습니다. "만약 내가 어제 꾸었던 꿈을 네가 꾸었다면 넌 그렇게 이야기하지 않을걸. 사실, 너도 거기 있었어. 진짜 너는 아니었지만, 당연히, 하지만 꿈속의 너 말이야. 꽤 무서웠어."

그는 자신의 침대 밑에서 신발 상자를 꺼냈습니다.

"여기 있어." 버스터가 말했습니다. "너 이거 받아."

"왜?"

"화석이 안에 들어 있어. 네가 전에 이거 보고 싶다고 말했잖아. 이제 네가 이걸 가져도 돼."

page 58

"버스터, 나도 화석을 원하지 않아. 이건 옳지 않아."

버스터가 자신의 눈을 비볐습니다. "난 이걸 없애야 해, 아서. 난 미쳐가고 있어."

아서는 방을 한 번 더 둘러보았습니다. "그래 그런 것 같아." 그가 말했습니다.

"난 엄청 좋을 줄 알았어, 백만 년이나 된 것을 나 혼자 갖고 있는 게 말이야. 나는 내가 마치 특별하고 중요하게 느껴질 줄 알았어. 그렇지만 내가 느끼는 것은 단지..."

"죄책감?"

버스터는 앞뒤로 서성거렸습니다. "모르겠어. 그렇지만 그게 나를 미치게 하고 있어, 그건 확실하지. 난 더 이상 그걸 쳐다볼 수도 없을 정도야."

아서는 상자를 바라보았습니다. "화석은 여기나 우리 집에도 어울리지 않아." 그가 말했습니다. "너도 알고 있듯이."

버스터는 한숨을 쉬었습니다. "그래서 그게 도대체 어디에 속하는데?"

아서가 그에게 시선을 던졌습니다. "네가 나한테 말해 봐." 그가 말했습니다.

10장

page 59

레인보우 록 방문자 센터 안에서, 아서

와 버스터는 불안해하며 문 옆에 서 있었습니다.

"그들이 너무 오래 걸려." 버스터가 말했습니다. 그는 자신의 두 손을 마주 비볐습니다. "어쩌면 우리는 오지 말았어야 했는지도 몰라."

아서는 미소를 지어보려고 했습니다. "자자, 그 *이야기*를 또 시작하지는 말자고..."

버스터는 앞뒤로 서성거렸습니다. "나도 어쩔 수 없어." 그가 말했습니다. "나는 기다리는 걸 잘하지 못한단 말이야. 넌 무슨 문제가 있다고 생각하니?"

"물론 그렇지 않았으면 해." 아서가 말했습니다.

page 60

마침내, 루스 대원이 그들에게 다가왔습니다. 고생물학자 직원 가운데 한 명도 그녀와 함께였습니다.

"안녕, 얘들아." 그녀가 말했습니다. "다시 보게 되어서 기쁘구나."

"저희도 여기에 와서 기뻐요." 아서가 말했습니다. 그는 버스터를 불안하게 바라보았습니다. "그렇지 않니?"

버스터가 고개를 끄덕였습니다. "그래서, 우리한테 말해주실 수 있는 게 뭔가요?" 그는 흥분해서 물었습니다.

루스 대원이 팔짱을 꼈습니다. "아무 결정도 내려지지 않았어."

아서는 한숨 쉬었습니다.

"무엇보다, 우리는 아직 확신할 수가 없구나." 고생물학자가 말했습니다.

"아직도요?" 버스터가 말했습니다. 그와 아서가 루스 대원에게 화석을 돌려준 지가 꼬박 한 달이 되었습니다. 그들은 그녀를 두가지 이유로 놀라게 했습니다. 그 화석이 희귀했기 때문이기도 했고 버스터가 애초에 그것을 공원에서 가져갔었기 때문입니다. 그러나 그녀는 그가 그것을 돌려주어서 기뻐했습니다. 그리고 그녀가 그의 악몽에 대해 들었을 때, 그녀는 그를 봐주기로 했습니다.

page 61

고생물학자는 미소 지었습니다. "난 네가 어떻게 느낄지 알아, 버스터. 안타깝게도, 이러한 것들은 시간이 걸린단다. 우리는 스펙트럼 분석, 방사성 탄소 연대측정을 해야 해..."

"알아요, 알아요." 버스터가 말했습니다. "과학을 서두를 수는 없죠. 그렇지만 저는 *제가* 화석이 되기 전에 결정이 나기를 바라고 있었어요."

"우리는 점점 더 가까워지고 있단다." 고생물학자가 말했습니다. "마쉬 박사님은 너희의 화석이 다스플레토사우루스 새끼의 발자국이라고 생각한단다. 코프 박사님은, 그렇지만, 이게 성장한 코엘루로사우르라고 생각하지."

"선생님은 어떻게 생각하세요?" 아서

가 물었습니다.

"난 너희 둘이 애초에 이 화석을 찾았다는 것부터가 멋지다고 생각한단다."

버스터가 활짝 웃었습니다. "많이 살펴봐야 했어요." 그는 생각하려고 잠시 멈추었습니다. "가능성은 거의 없었어요. 다행히, 우리는 우리의 도구들을 가지고 왔어요. 피스 헬멧은 특히 도움이 많이 되었어요. 아서가 그것을 들어 올렸을 때 전 화석을 분명하게 볼 수 있었거든요. 그렇지 않았다면, 전 그것을 놓쳤을 거예요."

page 63

"놓치지 않는 것에 대해 말이 나온김에," 루스 대원이 말했습니다. "나는 너희에게 뭔가를 보여주고 싶구나."

그녀는 전시장으로 그들을 데리고 걸어갔습니다.

발자국 화석 옆에는 황동으로 된 명판이 있었습니다. 그것은 공룡 발자국, 버스터 백스터와 아서 리드에 의해 발견됨이라고 쓰여 있었습니다.

"와!" 버스터가 말했습니다. "우리만의 명판이네요."

"내 이름이 이렇게 멋지게 보인 적은 없었어요." 아서가 말했습니다.

"내 생각에 이건 금인 것 같아요." 버스터가 말했습니다. 그가 잠시 말을 멈췄습니다. "하지만 이게 얼마나 오래 저기에 있을 수 있는 거죠?"

"화석이 남아있는 만큼 오래 있을 거야." 루스 대원이 말했습니다.

버스터는 미소 지었습니다. "그건 제게는 충분히 긴 시간이에요." 그가 말했습니다.

Chapter 1

1. B They were riding in a school bus entering Rainbow Rock State Park. The class had come there for a field trip.

2. A The park was a great place to hunt for fossils of ancient animals—including dinosaurs.

3. D Binky leapt out onto the pavement. He clawed at the air. "*T. rex.* Grrr!" Francine lowered her head at him and stamped her foot. "Triceratops. Raarrr!"

4. A And today he had come specially prepared. Unlike the others, who were wearing their regular clothes, he had dressed very carefully. "Isn't that hat hot?" Arthur asked. Buster shook his head. "It's not a hat—it's a pith helmet. This is what paleontologists ear. It keeps them cool under the hot desert sun."

5. C "You'll thank me later. We don't want to be caught unprepared. Hey, where did we put the chisels?" "I've got them," said Arthur. "What about the field guides?" "Got those, too." "Oooh! I hope we didn't forget—" "Don't worry," said Arthur, patting his side pocket. "I have the brushes right here."

Chapter 2

1. D "Oh, good. A volunteer. Now, don't be shy. What do you think a fossil is?" Buster took a deep breath. "Fossils are the calcified remains of ancient organisms. Minerals seep into these organisms' tissues and harden, preserving their original forms."

2. C "Well, well, well!" Ranger Ruth looked stunned. "Count on me to pick out the class genius. Moving right along, we have a little show for you to see. LIGHTS!" As the lights dimmed in the room, a spotlight shined on the dinosaur diorama.

3. A Then the dragonfly collapsed, and the brachiosaurus split apart, the front end remaining on the stage while the back end ran off. Everyone laughed.

4. D Ranger Ruth spoke into a microphone. "A hundred million years ago, Rainbow Rock State Park looked very different. It was much hotter. There were lots of ferns." … "And, of course, there were dinosaurs." "Much much later,

this whole area was covered by the sea. Over millions of years, the soil turned to rock. And the bones and shells turned to rock, too."

5. C   A spotlight was switched on, revealing a giant brachiosaurus skeleton on the far side of the hall.

Chapter 3

1. C   "Now, the top layers are from about twenty million years later," the ranger continued. "So we can tell how old a fossil is by noting where it was found in the cliff."

2. B   "Don't worry," said Ranger Ruth. "The cliffs are for the professional paleontologists. You kids will hunt in the stream."

3. D   "Oh. Well, we're going to break for a snack now, and then we'll be heading back to the bus."

4. A   "Are you sure you're feeling okay, Buster? I've never seen you turn down food before."

5. B   Buster did. The stone showed an imprint with a three-pronged indentation. "Oh, wow," said Arthur. "It's a leaf fossil."

Chapter 4

1. B   Buster shook his head again. He was too excited to eat or drink. He was having enough trouble just breathing. Imagine! He had found a real dinosaur fossil.

2. B   Ranger Ruth brushed a few cookie crumbs off her shirt. "I think everyone worked up quite an appetite," she said. "While you finish up, let's go around and talk about the fossils we found."

3. C   Buster blinked. "Wait a minute!" he cried. "Can't we all keep what we found?" Ranger Ruth shook her head. "Oh, I'm sorry. Maybe you weren't listening when I explained earlier. We put as many fossils as we can in the museum so everyone can have a chance to see them." "And you include proper credit," said the Brain. "Absolutely," said the ranger.

4. A The ranger examined them. "Yes, they are. Streaks of mica and quartz, I believe. I think I'll hold on to them for further study." Francine beamed. "See that," she said to Muffy. "Further study. I found important rocks."

5. A "Do you boys have something to add?" the ranger asked. "Did our budding expert find anything he'd like to share?" "Nothing," said Buster. "Nothing at all."

Chapter 5

1. C Arthur wasn't in the mood to play dinosaur. He was nervous.

2. B "I'm not giving it up," said Buster. He squeezed the fossil gently. "It's like holding a piece of history." "But what if they search us on the way out? We could get arrested! What if they have some special fossil-detector alarm?"

3. A "Well, that doesn't make me feel better," said Arthur. "Remember, the time Muffy brought goat cheese to class and you insisted it was fake—because you had never heard of it?" "That was different," said Buster. "It doesn't make sense that goats can make cheese if all they eat are tin cans."

4. A "Uh-oh," said Arthur. "Look, Buster, Ranger Ruth is coming toward us. She's going to frisk us. I told you this would happen. But did you want to listen? Noooooo. They must have some kind of detector hidden in the trees. It's probably triggered by an infrared—"

5. C "You look a little uncomfortable," said the ranger. She patted Buster on the back. "I hope you're not too discouraged about your fossil hunting. You have the makings of a real paleontologist."

Chapter 6

1. A "Well, who *can* we tell?" Arthur asked. "Nobody. We have to keep it a secret."

2. C When Buster got home, he went straight to his room. He closed the door and pulled down his window shade. "Perimeter security in place," he said. Next, he wrapped the fossil in tinfoil. Then he put it inside a plastic bag and put

the bag in a shoe box. "Phase One complete." He filled the rest of the shoe box with marbles from a bowl and put it on a shelf in his closet.

3. B "What's that you've done to your mashed potatoes?" his mother asked. Buster looked down at his plate. "It kind of looks like a dinosaur footprint," his mother went on.

4. D "No, I'm not," said the dinosaur. "Maybe you think you can ignore me because I'm not that big. Don't be fooled. I have big and powerful friends." The dinosaur flicked his tail behind him. Buster saw a tyrannosaurus and a triceratops standing there. The tyrannosaurus, though, had Binky's head, and the triceratops had Francine's.

5. B "We're coming!" said the voices outside. "We want the footprint!"

Chapter 7

1. D "The worst part," said Buster, "was that Binky's head looked so natural on top of the tyrannosaurus."

2. C "True," said Arthur. "But don't you think your dream was trying to tell you something?" Buster considered it. "Yes, it was telling me not to put so much chocolate sauce on my apple pie. I think I got a little stomachache before bedtime."

3. A Arthur sighed. "So when can I come over and see it?" "You can't. No one can."

4. D Buster was saved from trying to answer that question because Francine was on her way over. "Good morning, Arthur. You look kind of tired, Buster. Didn't sleep well, huh? Probably feeling bad because you didn't find anything yesterday."

5. D "Or, even rarer, dinosaur footprints. Wouldn't that have been exciting?" Everyone nodded.

Chapter 8

1. B Buster jumped off his bed. "Okay? Of course, I'm okay. Why wouldn't I be okay? Don't I look okay?" His mother wasn't so sure. "Well, you look a little

tired. You're not having any problems at school, are you?"

2. D "Hi," said Arthur. "I had a question about our math homework. Are we supposed to measure things by the *foot* or the *meter*?" "*Foot*? What makes you say *foot*?" "How else should I say it?" Arthur asked. "You don't fool me," said Buster. "You know perfectly well we're supposed to do both. You're just checking up on my *you-know-what*."

3. C He found his mother holding the shoe box. "What's this, Buster? It feels kind of heavy." "That?" Buster rushed over and took it out of her hand. "It's a school project. Very delicate. Hush-hush. Top secret. Can't talk about it now."

4. B *The door burst open. Ranger Ruth and a police officer entered. They were dragging Arthur behind them. He was wearing a striped prisoner's uniform.*

5. A *The ranger laughed. "We have reason to believe you're hiding a dinosaur in this room."*

Chapter 9

1. D Buster was absent from school the next day. Arthur wasn't really worried because he figured that Buster was just sick. But he decided to go by the Baxters' apartment on his way home.

2. C Arthur blinked. The room was a mess. Everything had been emptied out of the closet, and there was a web of string crisscrossing the room.

3. A "But Buster, dinosaurs have been extinct for millions of years. You know that." "I think that's just what they want us to believe. It's all part of their master plan." "Their master plan?" Buster nodded. "That's why they've left all those fossils to find. They want to trick us. But I'm not fooled. I'm going to be ready."

4. B "I thought it would be so great, having this million-year-old thing to myself. I thought I would feel special and important. But all I feel is . . ." "Guilty?"

5. D Arthur stared at the box. "The fossil doesn't belong here or at my house," he said. "You know that."

Chapter 10

1. B "Basically, we're just not sure yet," said the paleontologist. "Still?" said Buster. It had been a whole month since he and Arthur had "Basically, we're just not sure yet," said the paleontologist. "Still?" said Buster. It had been a whole month since he and Arthur had returned the fossil to Ranger Ruth.

2. C They had surprised her, both because the fossil was rare and because Buster had taken it from the park in the first place. But she was pleased that he had returned it.

3. A And when she heard about his nightmares, she decided to go easy on him.

4. D He stopped to think. "The odds were against us. Luckily, we had brought our tools. The pith helmet especially helped a lot. I could see the fossil clearly when Arthur held it up. I might have missed it otherwise."

5. C "Speaking of not missing things," said Ranger Ruth, "I want to show you something." She walked them over to the display case. Next to the fossil footprint was a brass plaque. It read *Dinosaur Footprint, Discovered by Buster Baxter and Arthur Read.*

버스터의 공룡 대소동
(Buster's Dino Dilemma)

1판 1쇄   2015년 10월 12일
1판 5쇄   2020년 8월 7일

지은이   Marc Brown
기획   이수영
책임편집   김보경 정소이
콘텐츠제작및감수   롱테일북스 편집부
저작권   김보경
마케팅   김보미 정경훈

펴낸이   이수영
펴낸곳   (주)롱테일북스
출판등록   제2015-000191호
주소   04043 서울특별시 마포구 양화로 12길 16-9(서교동) 북앤빌딩 3층
전자메일   helper@longtailbooks.co.kr
(학원 · 학교에서 본도서를 교재로 사용하길 원하시는 경우 전자메일로 문의주시면
자세한 안내를 받으실 수 있습니다.)

ISBN 979-11-86701-03-4 14740

롱테일북스는 (주)북하우스 퍼블리셔스의 계열사입니다.

이 도서의 국립중앙도서관 출판시도서목록(CIP)은 서지정보유통지원시스템 홈페이지(http://seoji.nl.go.kr)와
국가자료공동목록시스템(http://www.nl.go.kr/kolisnet)에서 이용하실 수 있습니다. (CIP 제어번호 : CIP2015025777)